JAMES

James

The Righteous Life That God Desires

Charles R. Tyree

CHRISTIAN PUBLICATIONS
CAMP HILL, PENNSYLVANIA

Christian Publications
3825 Hartzdale Drive
Camp Hill, PA 17011
www.cpi-horizon.com

Faithful, biblical publishing since 1883

ISBN: 0-87509-781-2

99 00 01 02 03 5 4 3 2 1

Contents

Acknowledgments

I must acknowledge the contributions of several of God's choice servants to the writing of this commentary on James. First, I owe Dr. Elio Cuccaro a great debt of gratitude for the generous investment of his time and mentoring influence as the editor of this series of commentaries. His assistance has been of great importance to me. Dr. Robert Traina and Dr. Robert Lyon are two men God has used to shape my understanding of exegesis and to intensify my love for God's Word.

I must thank the people and leadership of the Greenfield, Massachusetts and Vineland, New Jersey Christian and Missionary Alliance churches for their patience in allowing me time to work on this project. Their input was crucial as I preached my way through the book of James in their pulpits.

My wife Sharon patiently read through every page of this material and offered her literary gifts to God for the writing of the commentary. I am thankful to God for her and for my children, Ryan and Elise, for their patience while I worked and their incentive for me to live the righteous life that God desires.

Lesson 1

James 1:1-5

Section A

(Introduction) Modeled by the Author

James 1:1

James, a servant of God and of the Lord Jesus Christ,
To the twelve tribes scattered among the nations.

Every age of Christianity has a challenge: God's people need a word from the Lord to answer their questions. The New Testament letter written by James meets that challenge. In the case of this letter, some of the questions of God's people specifically concerned how the saints should handle suffering. But the letter goes on to cover controlling our communications and connecting faith with faithfulness to God. Even the struggle of wealthy and poor believers to relate to one another in love and our hunger for prayer that truly communicates with God are addressed in this brief letter.

Every believer's search for wisdom, true righteousness and faith in the context of our age and cultures is rewarded in the book of James. The "nuts and bolts" of the deeper life come together here to build a sanctified man or woman who really functions as a spiritually mature believer in the midst of a broken world.

Who Is James?

Six or seven New Testament characters bear the name James. Which one wrote this epistle? Overwhelmingly, church fathers and biblical scholars over the centuries credit "James the Just, the Lord's brother" as the author of this letter.[1] James was the leader of the church in Jerusalem from the first days of its inception. We see him in Acts 12:17; 15:13 and 21:18 as the spokesman and leader of the Jerusalem Council. His authority gave him the chair of the Council as the Gentile mission of Paul was considered and approved.

In Acts 15:13-21, James made the final judgment in the Jerusalem Council concerning what would be required of Gentile believers for them to be accepted into the church. James received the report of Peter's miraculous escape from prison and of Paul's missionary journey. He held the highest office in the most influential church in history.

James and the rest of the elders supported the work of Paul but expressed their concerns about rumors that Paul was teaching Jewish believers that they did not need to obey the customs of the Jewish faith. In each case, James was the champion for faith in Christ and also for Jewish believers to be held accountable to the standards of the Mosaic law. Just as Christ called

Paul to define the faith in Gentile terms, the Lord seems to have given James the calling of detailing the life He intended for Judaic Christians.

A James is also identified in the Gospels and in Paul's writing as one of the brothers of the Lord (Matthew 13:55; Mark 6:3; Galatians 1:19).[2] James initially doubted that Jesus was the Christ and later came to believe. His emphasis on the nature of true faith illuminates what happened to change the man whom John 7:5 reports as unbelieving: "For even [Jesus'] own brothers did not believe in him."

Early traditions about James suggest that he was the first one to whom the Lord appeared after the resurrection and that he prayed so much that he had calluses on his knees like a camel. Hegesippus, quoted in Eusebius,[3] recorded that James, known as "the Just," had taken the vow of a Nazarite and was martyred by the Jews by being thrown from the pinnacle of the Temple and then stoned.

Josephus spoke of James as the Lord's brother, of his martyrdom and the ensuing judgment on the city of Jerusalem.[4] James had a reputation in the writing of the church fathers for being a righteous, holy man of God.

James was also a devout Jew. In spite of his special relationship to the Lord and his high position in the Church, James identifies himself simply as "a servant of God and of the Lord Jesus Christ." For such an important man to take upon himself the title of a slave must be noted as unusual by a world so driven by position and power. It is also remarkable that a devout Jew would mention God and Jesus Christ equally in his opening greeting.[5] Christ was the Lord of Jewish Christianity, and James was the servant of the One whom he had come to believe and trust for eternal life.

Whom Does the Letter Address?

James is writing to "the twelve tribes scattered among the nations." James is a Jew writing to suffering and oppressed Jewish believers scattered by persecution.[6] He refers to "our ancestor Abraham" in James 2:21 and calls his readers "brothers" eleven times (1:2; 2:1, 14; 3:1, 10, 12; 4:11; 5:7, 10, 12, 19). The practical pastoral thrust of the letter speaks to a generation which had grown up under the legalistic umbrella of the Pharisees and Sadducees, whose message and methods the content of James condemns.[7] James echoes the teachings of Jesus Christ regarding the nature of true righteousness and acceptable religion (i.e., Matthew 5-7 and 23).

James is not writing as an evangelist and missionary like Paul or as an evangelist to the Jewish people like Peter. Rather, he is writing as a pastor to first-century believers, primarily to those who had come to Christ from Judaism, and to subsequent generations of Christians, teaching the nature of "the righteous life that God desires" (James 1:20).

James proclaims the difference between worthless religion and "religion that God our Father accepts as pure and faultless" (1:27). Just as the apostle Paul defines faith for the Gentile believer, James defines the meaning of Christianity for the Jewish believer. Rather than conflicting, their writings complement one another. By looking at both James' and Paul's letters, we can more completely understand the many facets of the Christian life.

Although the letter is infused with doctrine, its purpose is to lead the church into the sanctified life which Christ intends His disciples to live rather than to explain doctrine.[8] As the leader of the church, the "bishop of Jerusalem" worked daily to correct the prejudices and misconceptions of the flock under his care. Faith in Christ had given James, like Paul, a new understanding of righteousness, faith in God, wisdom and wealth. No longer bound by Jewish tradition, he rejected the simulated righteousness of legalistic religion and proclaimed the "perfect law that gives freedom" (1:25).

The letter he wrote gives flesh and muscle to the expression of Christian love, faith and wisdom. Against the backdrop of persecution and suffering, the message of true righteousness and hope in the promises of God must have been a great encouragement to the Jews who read this powerful letter.

A rare piece of historical evidence helps us to place the letter we are reading into its historical context. Josephus, a first-century historian, reported that James was tried by the Sanhedrin under the leadership of high priest Ananus II. In a three- or four-month interval in A.D. 62, this high priest decided to take the opportunity of the absence of a Roman procurator to rid Jerusalem of a number of popular leaders who did not support his patriotic Jewish agenda. James was martyred during this time.[9]

James' appeal to reject anger and live "the righteous life that God desires" (1:20) and his later appeals for "patience in the face of suffering" (5:10) indicate that James had actually gotten involved in the conquest for a spiritual kingdom—and not a political one as he was accused of doing. First-century Middle Eastern culture—seething political upheaval, the inception of intense persecution of the Church and the initial tension between Jewish tradition and Christian doctrine—is the boiling, tumultuous backdrop of this essential letter.

How Does James Apply to the Present Church?

True holiness, expressed in the life God created each new Christian to live, is at a premium in every age. Churches are filled with mediocre disciples who say and believe one thing mentally while their conduct reveals a much lower standard. James led the church, but not by virtue of his "connections" to the Lord or his credentials as a man of great integrity and reputation. Instead, his leadership was based upon a self-concept revealed in the first verse of the letter. The call of God to be a servant of the Lord Jesus Christ moved his pen as the words were formed for the letter.

The book of James can refocus our generation of Christians. The truth of the letter should move us away from overemphasis upon what the Church believes to a new focus on how the Church behaves. The disparity between the beliefs of today's Christians and their daily actions and attitudes is alarming.[10]

This split personality in the Church is not the life Jesus described: "I tell you the truth, anyone who has faith in me will do what I have been doing. He will do even greater things than these" (John 14:12).

The deeper life described in James is the Christ-life. Although James did not mention the work of the Holy Spirit to produce this sanctified life, he clearly understood that God is the Source of every grace the believer enjoys (1:16-18; 2:17; 3:5-7). The reader must connect the practical instruction of James with the prayer of Paul that we will receive power from the Holy Spirit to first understand and then apply the truth of God's loving plan (Ephesians 3:14-21) to our daily lives. The sanctifying power of God is available (1 Thessalonians 5:23-24) to any who will hear the message of James and launch out by faith to make his word their compass. My hope and prayer is that God will use the words of James to transform His Church once again, and that He will begin with us.

Section B

Developed by Persevering Faith

James 1:2-4

Consider it pure joy, my brothers, whenever you face trials of many kinds, because you know that the testing of your faith develops perseverance. Perseverance must finish its work so that you may be mature and complete, not lacking anything.

While visiting a working gold mine in Colorado, I paid $1 for a golf ball-sized lump of gold ore and a small card identifying me as an official "little miner." The tour guide told us how many tons of the rock must be superheated to the melting point in order to produce just a few ounces of pure gold.

James is making a similar point in the beginning of his letter to suffering believers. To make gold, you must have a fire. In order to produce mature, Christlike people, God uses a spiritual smelting process involving "trials of many kinds." No other process will refine and purify our lives to the point of maturity in the faith. The result is so precious to God and to the individual believer that God is willing to allow this process to be repeated throughout the Christian life until the refining is complete and the life is pure and holy.

Faith Perseveres with Joy (1:2)

Each Christian will face difficulties. These various internal and external troubles will come upon us unpredictably. These are "whenever" events; they follow no discernible pattern. Our Lord predicted similar things for His followers in His Sermon on the Mount:

> Blessed are you who are poor,
> for yours is the kingdom of God.
> Blessed are you who hunger now,
> for you will be satisfied.
> Blessed are you who weep now,
> for you will laugh.
> Blessed are you when men hate you,
> when they exclude you and insult you
> and reject your name as evil,
> because of the Son of Man.
>
> Rejoice in that day and leap for joy, because great is your reward in heaven. For that is how their fathers treated the prophets. (Luke 6:20-23)

Christ was tested in various ways in the wilderness and throughout His life among us (Hebrews 4:15). Trials should be the expectation of believers even when we are not facing the difficulties produced by our own sin.

"Trials of many kinds" (James 1:2) would indicate that the variety of sources of trouble is great. Although the trials experienced by James' readers may have been caused primarily by persecution, any circumstances that test the believer's faith would also be understood from this word "trials."[11] Trials are usually accompanied by "temptations to evil thoughts or actions," which happens to be one possible meaning of the word "trials" used here.[12]

The heating, melting and molding process has more than one step. Producing Christlikeness in fallen humans is a complicated and lifelong process. Passing one test should not lead us to believe we have graduated. While there is much joy in the Christian life, it is not intended to be an easy life. James views these various troubles as essential to our development and growth.[13]

The command to "consider it pure joy" when these events intrude upon our lives is a difficult one to apply. The word "consider" is used in other places in the New Testament to mean "to lead, guide."[14] This is a matter of intentional change in our attitude toward the troubles and difficulties of the Christian life. Trouble is rarely welcomed or easy, and natural attitudes and responses to trials will need to be reshaped. This new perspective requires believers to look beyond the present circumstances to the greater purpose God is achieving through testing.

"Pure joy" is superior to happiness because it is not driven by favorable circumstances. Booker T. Washington was familiar with trouble and suffering. He was a son of slaves, born on a Virginia plantation. He worked at the end of the nineteenth century in a salt furnace and in the coal mines with a pick and shovel. He was forced to seek education in the few places it was available for him. He said:

> No man should be pitied because every day of his life he faces a hard, stubborn problem. It is the man who has no problems to solve, no hard-

> ships to face, who is to be pitied. He has nothing in his life which will strengthen and form his character, nothing to call out his latent powers and deepen and widen his hold on life.[15]

God used these difficulties to form a man who was a leader to a generation.

Joy is the proper perspective for the test of faith.[16] Pure joy is taking pleasure in making progress in the deeper life as a member of Christ's kingdom. Paul said, "The kingdom of God is not a matter of eating and drinking, but of righteousness, peace and joy in the Holy Spirit" (Romans 14:17). Joy is the delight of the soul that springs from hope in God's loving purpose within difficult circumstances.

Faith Passes the Tests of Life (1:3)

"Why?" That is perhaps the most frequently asked question during a time of stress or pain. James gives an interesting pair of responses to this question in the statement beginning with the word "because" (1:3).

God works through our struggles to test our faith. "Faith" is trust in the person and character of God as revealed in the Word He has given to believers. Testing faith is like proof-testing metals to determine their purity and strength. These tests are the means of determining the relative strength and purity of believers.[17] James' readers now have a baseline measurement to determine how the refining process is going. What is the quality of their faith?

Scripture promises that our work while on this planet will all be tested by God. "His work will be shown for what it is, because the Day will bring it to light. It will be revealed with fire, and the fire will test the quality of each man's work" (1 Corinthians 3:13). That same day will be the final test of the faith God has produced in us throughout a lifetime.

A common Jewish and biblical image is the refiner's fire (e.g., Zechariah 13:9). As the refiner heats the ore, the impurities come to the surface to be skimmed away, leaving only the precious metal behind. God is refining the faith of His people so that it is pure and strong and precious.

The second reason given for this process of testing is that it "develops perseverance" (James 1:3). The New English Bible translates it "fortitude"; the Revised Standard Version says it is "steadfastness." Notice that this is something God produces through trouble and testing. Men will not develop this virtue by their own unaided efforts or without this process.

The loving purpose of God will take His people into and through trouble—like Abraham sacrificing Isaac, Job praising God through his suffering or Peter growing through the failure of a night spent denying his Lord—in order to develop perseverance in faith. The volatile and inconsistent Simon was hardened and tempered by these tests to become a "rock" of faith and consistency for Christ (Matthew 16:13-18). Paul mentioned this perseverance as an essential element of the Christian's character sixteen times. The book of Revelation stresses the need for persistent faithfulness and trust in Christ.

Perseverance is more than just patience in the midst of trouble. It is the ability to stand firm in faith for God.[18] Perseverance goes beyond enduring the various tests of life to passing them and bringing glory to God.

Faith Perfects the Character (1:4)

James depicts a progression: faith is refined in the heat of life's tests and trials in order to produce perseverance. But that is not the end of the refining process. God has another step in mind to produce another virtue and to complete the final precious product: "Perseverance must finish its work so that you may be mature and complete, not lacking anything" (1:4).

Life seems to be a whole collection of unfinished tasks. As we look around us, we see paintings that are partially completed, projects begun but never finished. I will always remember my neighbor the bricklayer whose home had brick only halfway up the front wall that faced our street. Unlike men, God is able to finish what He has begun. Perseverance can produce a life that is pleasing to God when it is not short-circuited by our impatience and lack of trust in God.

What is the goal? All this is "so that you may be mature and complete, not lacking anything" (1:4). Christians are actually intended to be enabled by God to live "the righteous life that God desires" (1:20). God intends to go beyond giving His people the self-control to act mature. He intends to enable us to *be* mature. This truth gives us the great hope that this process of refining has a reachable goal. God intends to make us pure gold through to the center of our being, unlike costume jewelry with a thin coating of gold on the outside.

What does it mean to be "mature and complete"? James lists no single virtue. God is looking for a balanced character, with every fruit of the Holy Spirit in place.[19] The loving Heavenly Refiner will not be finished with a man until he is a balanced illustration of the life of Christ expressed in the crucible of living. James will continue throughout this practical book to develop the description of the life God desires to produce.

Paul says in First Corinthians 13 that the greatest gifts are vain unless love is their motivation. Hebrews 11 teaches us that faith is essential to a life that is pleasing to God. James tells us here that God can give men a life "not lacking anything" (James 1:4). How? As Henri Nouwen has said, "Your life is not going to be easy, and it should not be easy. It ought to be hard. It ought to be radical; it ought to be restless; it ought to lead you to places you'd rather not go."[20] Within the guiding hand of a gracious God, such a life can perfect the character of a man, woman or child in Christ.

Conclusion

Rejoice in the trials and troubles of life. Faith perseveres with joy as it senses the hand of God refining life and producing gold in the fire of testing. Faith passes the tests of life as God develops character into a persevering metal that does not bend to the shape of the world or break in the time of suffering, but holds faithfully the image of Christ.

Faith perfects the character of the believer into a mature, complete representation of God's gracious purpose for His children. This is the process of God's sanctifying work in your life. Submit to the Refiner's fire. Don't run from trouble or rebel at the first sign of heat—trust God to use your trouble, your suffering, your frustrations, your disappointments and even your persecution to form you and purify your life.

Are you tempted to doubt God's love in the pain of illness or the frustration of unrealized dreams? Persevere in trusting God. Pray that as one of God's "little miners" you will stand the test of the fire and emerge by God's grace mature and complete in Christ.

Questions for Reflection or Discussion

1. Why do the tests, trials and sudden temptations we experience seem to surprise us? What are some other passages where Scripture predicts that Christians will suffer various kinds of suffering and persecution?
2. What is the secret to "pure joy" in the midst of life's trials? What role does the Holy Spirit play in transforming frustration or despair into joy? Can you name a believer who is a great example of joy in the midst of life's trials?
3. If God already knows how strong your faith is before the test, then what is the purpose of testing it?
4. According to James, how is the person who is "mature and complete, not lacking anything" developed?

Endnotes

1. Peter Davids, *The Epistle of James,* The New International Greek Testament Commentary (Grand Rapids: Eerdmans, 1982), 2.
2. Joseph B. Mayor, *The Epistle of James* (Grand Rapids: Kregel Publications, 1913, reprinted 1990), xi.
3. Eusebius, *Ecclesiastical History,* ii., 23.
4. Mayor, *Epistle of James,* lvi-lviii; citing Ant. Jud. xx. 9.1.
5. James Adamson, *The Epistle of James,* The New International Commentary on the New Testament (Grand Rapids: Eerdmans, 1976), 50-51.

6. Ralph P. Martin, *James,* Word Biblical Commentary (Waco, TX: Word, Inc., 1988), lxvii-lxix.
7. Adamson, *Epistle of James,* 34.
8. Ibid., 20.
9. Martin, *James,* lxii-lxvii.
10. George Barna, *The Frog in the Kettle* (Ventura, CA: Regal Books, 1990), 112-119.
11. James H. Ropes, *Saint James,* Critical and Exegetical Commentary Series (Edinburgh: T & T Clark, 1991), 132-133.
12. Martin, *James,* 11.
13. Davids, *Epistle of James,* 70.
14. William G. Arndt and F. Wilbur Gingrich, *A Greek-English Lexicon of the New Testament* (London: The University of Chicago Press, 1957), 344.
15. "Washington, Booker T." Microsoft® Encarta® Encyclopedia, 1995 ed.
16. Adamson, *Epistle of James,* 53.
17. Davids, *Epistle of James,* 68.
18. Martin, *James,* 16.
19. Mayor, *Epistle of James,* 346-347.
20. As quoted in *Leadership,* Winter 1996, vol. XVII, No. 1, 81.

Lesson 2

James 1:5-11

Section A

Invested in Prayer for Wisdom

James 1:5-8

If any of you lacks wisdom, he should ask God, who gives generously to all without finding fault, and it will be given to him. But when he asks, he must believe and not doubt, because he who doubts is like a wave of the sea, blown and tossed by the wind. That man should not think he will receive anything from the Lord; he is a double-minded man, unstable in all he does.

If you rub the magic lamp, the genie will grant you three wishes! The thought of such a fantasy has sparked the imagination of generations.

Jesus Christ asked the question, "What good is it for a man to gain the whole world, and yet lose or forfeit his very self?" (Luke 9:25). This section of James directs persecuted people with tremendously challenging lives to pray, to "ask God." But prayer is not like rubbing a magic lamp. Prayer requires faith. God demands that petitioners trust Him to answer—and to answer in a loving and wise way. The first, most critical need of every praying Christian is wisdom.

When You Pray, Ask God for Wisdom (1:5)

Wisdom—"the practical application of divine knowledge"[1]—is a gift from God. We all need it; we just fail to see our need. When King Solomon was invited by God to ask for anything he wanted, Solomon prayed for wisdom (1 Kings 3:5-15). Listen to the advice of Proverbs 4:5-7:

> Get wisdom, get understanding;
> do not forget my words or swerve from them.
> Do not forsake wisdom, and she will protect you;
> love her, and she will watch over you.
> Wisdom is supreme; therefore get wisdom.
> Though it cost all you have, get understanding.

Solomon did not pray for wealth, a long life, power, popularity or love. He prayed for the most essential thing! Without wisdom, we lack the ability to enjoy or to even manage the other blessings of life.

Wisdom is available only from God. Mankind has sought it through philosophy and science. We have depended upon our "common sense." But those things fail to give us the ability to apply the knowledge we have. For the Jewish mind, "wisdom" meant practical righteousness in everyday living.[2] Though we have more knowledge than any generation in history, we fail to live peacefully with one another or to make positive contributions to our generation.

Thomas Edison held the patents for dozens of inventions. But folklore has it that Edison claimed only one of his many inventions was his own idea. All the rest were simply reorganizations of other people's ideas! Spiritual wisdom is the result of knowledge plus a means to use it for God's glory. Only God can give man the ability to apply knowledge wisely so that it is positive rather than destructive.

And this wisdom is readily available from God. "If any of you lacks wisdom," the Bible promises, "he should ask God, who gives generously to all without finding fault" (James 1:5). Our lack of wisdom is not the fault of God. The Heavenly Father is willing and able to give this much-needed insight to His people—to anyone. The problem is that petitioners are often seeking solutions on their own terms rather than on His.

People unwisely decide to "lean on their own understanding" (see Proverbs 3:5) and to seek to meet their needs from a source other than God. We pray for money, gambling that money is really what is needed for happiness and spiritual development. We pray for perfect health, assuming that this will fulfill our need for the grace of God. But Paul needed a "thorn in the flesh" (see 2 Corinthians 12:7-10) in order to see God's strength made perfect in his weakness. Paul's problem was a part of God's wise plan for his life. James counsels, "Pray for wisdom first, and know that God will grant your request." He longs to impart this great gift.

God will give generously and without pausing to point out your deficiencies.[3] You will not get that parental lecture reminding you of how immature you really are. God grants your prayer request "sincerely and without mental reservation."[4]

But you must *ask!* Wisdom is not automatically granted to anyone. The current trials of this letter's readers were not necessarily a sign of God's displeasure with them, but were the invitation to growth and the experience of His grace.[5] The person who lacks God's insight into his situation, the church seeking direction, the nation that would govern its people wisely "should ask God . . . and it will be given" (James 1:5).

When You Pray for Wisdom, Believe in God (1:6)

"But when he asks . . ." For the believer, the scope of this praying is universal; God gives to all who will ask without regard for their merits, and His response is without any reservations.[6] The assumption here is that the person with the need, whatever it may be, will pray for wisdom. Although God is eager to grant such requests, there are some requirements for the life of the man or woman in prayer.

"But when he asks, he must believe . . ." (1:6). Christians have been confused by what it means to believe. We have thought that we are to believe in our prayers, insisting that God will answer them all by giving exactly what we demand without changing our order—like a good take-out restaurant. Or we have put faith in our faith: "If I just believe it hard enough, God will be forced to give me what I seek." Faith is not a means of manipulating God. Faith is trust in an all-wise, gracious and powerful Father. "And without faith it is impossible to please God, because anyone who comes to him must believe that he exists and that he rewards those who earnestly seek him" (Hebrews 11:6). Almighty God is the focus of our faith.

In a book titled *No God But God: Breaking with the Idols of Our Age,* Os Guinness and John Seel[7] point out that many people want to follow the course in life that will bring the most personal fulfillment, but they also wish to avoid being accountable to God. Men tend to make idols out of their own faith and their methodology in prayer, depending upon these things rather than upon God and His grace.

To trust in God is a matter of choice. "He must believe." We can choose to believe that God loves us as He has said. The cross of Christ is the evidence of this love. Or we may choose to believe that God does not love us, have our best interests in mind or know what is best for us. Such a lack of trust makes requests for wisdom futile.

When You Believe, Do Not Doubt God (1:6-8)

". . . he who doubts is like a wave of the sea, blown and tossed by the wind" (1:6). Waves do not choose anything about their existence. They are driven by the forces of their world, by every physical influence of their environment. The phases of the moon, tides, wind direction and velocity, prevailing currents like the Gulf Stream and even the passing of every ship distort their course. Using this image, James is alluding to a directionless life, where a person always vacillates between two or more opinions, never quite settled and able to make a straight course. There are many influencing forces in our world, all demanding that we believe in them with all our hearts. For the person who does not choose to trust God, prayer seems like just another way of covering all the bases.

When Moses went to the top of the mountain to hear God's wisdom, the people at the bottom of the mountain were praying too. But when their leader was delayed, they began to worship a god of their own making (Exodus 32). Rather than waiting for the wisdom of God and trusting in His ability to give them His revealed will, they impatiently trusted in their own wisdom. The results of this kind of unbelief are always disastrous—as they were for those who chose to align themselves with the idol of their own making.

"That man should not think he will receive anything from the Lord; he is a double-minded man, unstable in all he does" (James 1:7-8). Trusting God and anything or anyone else fails. Jesus said, "No one can serve two masters" (Matthew 6:24). Being "double-minded" is being half committed. It is like having two hearts, two loves[8]—having a "soul divided between two worlds."[9]

Loving God while loving my sin, my own opinion or my own desires creates a life that is self-contradictory. Loving one is hating the other. The whole Word of God demands single-hearted devotion to a sovereign God. James' readers were in the midst of testing and in the heat of persecution. The temptation to half-trust God and to half-trust in their own devices to deliver them or to make them happy was strongest when life was most difficult.

We often want both our sin *and* our relationship with God. Like King David, we want Bathsheba *and* the joy of our salvation. Like Ananias and Sapphira

(Acts 5), we want our money *and* the prestige of being considered generous. So we lie to ourselves, believing we can follow God and disobey Him at the same time. People pray but their prayers are unanswered.

Why does this surprise us? Many believers are angry when they pray and pray without any apparent results. We attend church services and perhaps even serve God in some ministry. But, as George Gallup discovered in one of his famous polls, those who believe in Christ also report that their beliefs do not always affect their choices.[10] His research revealed that modern Christians also love questionable movies, seek to gain some tax credits they are not actually entitled to and bend God's rules for relationships to include false ideas like "it's all right as long as you love the person." Faith in God's plan for living an abundant holy life is only an occasional experience.

"That man should not think he will receive anything from the Lord" (James 1:7). Faith produces a level of faithfulness, a righteous, holy way of life. Unbelief produces spiritual inconsistency, likened here to a constantly moving ocean of values and behaviors. A divided heart makes a person "unstable in all he does" (1:8). James began his letter seeing himself as a slave of God and of the Lord Jesus Christ. He sees every Christian as his brother or sister, his fellow slaves with a common Lord. Our Lord and Master will not reward unbelief and inconsistency with answered prayers.

Conclusion

The Christian life is intended to be one of stability because it is based upon God's wisdom for living. But when men choose to be double-minded, they find that their whole lives become a stormy sea. Nothing works—relationships are unstable; work is turmoil; churches are shaken loose from their moorings by storms of conflict and waves of confusion when divided allegiances destroy the unity of those with a once-steady faith.

When we pray, we must be single-minded in our trust in God alone, and if we do, we will see two results: a stability that comes from the powerful combination of wisdom and faith and effective prayer that God honors with wisdom and grace. This prayer of faith for wisdom from God is a daily characteristic of the deeper life.

When you pray, ask God for wisdom. Every circumstance of life and every new bit of knowledge requires the wisdom of God to apply it in a constructive way. When you pray, believe in God. Do not trust in your faith or in your knowledge, your abilities or your past experience. Trust a loving, gracious heavenly Father to know what you need and when you need it; seek His wisdom to understand your situation. When you believe in God, do not doubt. Being double-minded leads to failure, a life of stormy conflict and a fruitless prayer life. God's wisdom, discovered in patient prayer and anchored by a determined trust in the Lord, leads to peace and stability.

Questions for Reflection or Discussion

1. Does it seem odd to you that people who were suffering different kinds of tests and experiencing persecution would be commanded to pray for wisdom instead of, for instance, deliverance? Why is wisdom essential to people in trouble?

2. Where does the world around us look for wisdom? Where does James direct us to seek it? What kind of wisdom is available from science and philosophy? from God?
3. Do you really believe that God will give wisdom to anyone who asks Him? Why or why not? What is implied by the idea that God will give wisdom generously to any who ask?
4. Why is faith essential for effective prayer? What kind of faith does James have in mind? How is this different from other kinds of "faith"?
5. What does a person do when he is doubting God? How does a "double-minded man" live his life? use his money? use his time? In what ways are you double-minded? What is the cure for this instability?
6. What should the person with an inconsistent Christian life expect when he prays? What should the person leading a consistent life of faith and righteousness expect? Where does grace fit in?

Section B

Ennobled by God's Provision

James 1:9-11

The brother in humble circumstances ought to take pride in his high position. But the one who is rich should take pride in his low position, because he will pass away like a wild flower. For the sun rises with scorching heat and withers the plant; its blossom falls and its beauty is destroyed. In the same way, the rich man will fade away even while he goes about his business.

After praying for wisdom, it is possible to recognize the hand of God directing our lives. The second half of this lesson acknowledges God's providential care of His people as they live out a life of faith in the wisdom of God. Such a life permits a legitimate form of pride.

What are you proud of? Many of us are proud of our car, home, family, position, clothes, appearance or education. Some are proud of their humility! We all seem to have some "trophies" around the house. They can be actual plaques, blue ribbons, awards and medals, or they can be things that are represented by the photographs on the wall in the family room.

James is about to tell believers what they can be legitimately proud of. While one form of pride is a sin to be avoided, the following expressions of pride are virtues to be developed.

Take Pride in Your Temporal Poverty (1:9)

As the friendly form of address, "brother," indicates, Christians are the focus of the command that follows. Specifically, James begins with a word to Christians who find themselves in "humble circumstances." Jewish Christians were facing economic persecution, being forced out of the synagogue and becoming impoverished by their circumstances (John 9:22; 12:42). Here James introduces for the first time in his letter the recurring theme of wealth and poverty.

Some theorize that the church leader is addressing Christians as the people in "humble circumstances" and nonbelievers as those who have more wealth and status.[11] James may also be introducing wealth and poverty as tests of true faith and perseverance in the life of believers.[12] Wherever material wealth is the focus of Christians' lives, the danger of being "double-minded" (James 1:2-8) instead of mature Christians who please God is great.

Poverty in the world is one issue that every generation has had difficulty dealing with. The world's goods and honors are unevenly distributed, even in the church. Some have assumed that God's provision is based upon His love—"the more you have of power and possessions, the more you are loved by God." Others, equally confused by passages like this one, have assumed that poverty is actually a sign of being spiritual and Christlike (see Matthew 5:3; Luke 6:24).

Scripture teaches that much poverty is actually the result of man's sin. Proverbs teaches that sins like laziness, greed and drunkenness are causes of poverty (see also Proverbs 6:10-11; 11:24; 21:17; 23:21; 28:19). The Bible also portrays the careless disregard for God's requirements for generosity and sharing as a cause of poverty in the world (Luke 16:19-31). In these cases, it is no more noble to be poor than to be wealthy or middle-income.

The financial status of the believer may cloud his application of this Scripture. While many of us consider ourselves to be low-income or middle-income as we compare our status with others in our own culture, we must realize that all of us in the Western world are in the wealthiest ten percent of the world's population. Compared to the majority of believers in the Third World, we are better described by "the one who is rich." We are more like the rich young ruler who failed to follow Jesus (18:23) or the man who refused to help poor Lazarus (16:19) than like these persecuted Christians of the first century. But since the perception of wealth and poverty is subjective, most will identify with the Christian referred to in James 1:9.

"Humble circumstances" signifies a lack of status, the absence of material superiority.[13] The focus is on believers who lack the power, prestige and possessions to be considered important by the world. With value placed upon outward things, these believers might be tempted to feel sorry for themselves. In fact, the tendency to be ashamed of our lack of world-driven status is a temptation all the "have-nots" of the world can relate to.

But James commands the brother in such humble circumstances to refuse to be humiliated. In fact, he tells him that he "ought to take pride in his high position." To what high position is he referring? Every believer, every brother in Christ, is a "child of God," "coworker of Christ," "priest," "saint." Every descriptive title for the follower of Christ is one of immense honor. In terms of spiritual wealth, each believer is going to inherit all the riches of heaven in Christ. Jesus said that the meek will inherit the earth (Matthew 5:5).

Listen to the words of John describing the believer's position in Christ:

> How great is the love the Father has lavished on us, that we should be called children of God! And that is what we are! . . . Dear friends, now we are children of God, and what we will be has not yet been made known. But we know that when he appears, we shall be like him, for we shall see him as he is. (1 John 3:1-2)

No higher position on earth is possible. To be, along with James, "a servant of God and of the Lord Jesus Christ" (James 1:1) is the greatest honor a human can aspire to. The command to take pride in this position is suddenly understandable. Although pride can be evil (see 4:6), Christians are to have a righteous pride in God's provision for us. As James Adamson has said, "the moral quality of the exulting joy depends on its occasion."[14]

Paul used this word for pride more than thirty times to recommend taking pride in God's blessings. One example occurs in Second Corinthians 12:9: "But he said to me, 'My grace is sufficient for you, for my power is made perfect in weakness.' Therefore I will boast all the more gladly about my weaknesses, so that Christ's power may rest on me."

To give glory to God for the spiritual wealth of being a brother or sister in Christ rightly identifies the blessings of God. God's rich provision in Christ ennobles the life of the individual believer in spite of his low worldly status. For James, the eschatological reality of the blessings believers have "already but not yet" is always in mind.[15] Their rich inheritance is both a present reality of the deeper life and a future hope. In this elevated position, these humble people can take legitimate pride.[16]

Take Pride in Temporal Plenty (1:10)

With great deftness, the author shifts our attention to the person in the opposite set of circumstances. Expanding on "But the one who is rich," James continues to develop the theme of Christians' attitudes toward material status and wealth (cf. 1 Timothy 6:6-10, 17-19).

The tendency to seek to apply this verse only to those outside the faith[17] would rob the wealthy Christian reader of the important message James delivers here. The "brother" in James 1:9 can also refer to "the one who is rich" mentioned in 1:10.[18] The focus of James is upon correcting the problems he finds among believers in the church, not those in a lost world.[19] The wealthy believer must also know how to live "the righteous life that God desires" (1:20).

Although we don't see ourselves as "rich" as long as we can see someone else who has more than we do materially, the adjective is descriptive of all believers, as James has just observed. Even many of those living at the poverty level in the United States at the end of the twentieth century are rich in comparison to our brothers and sisters in Third World churches around the globe.

Rich Christians and poor Christians must not only compare their relative status in the world, but we must also contrast our attitude toward that status. Wealth or the lack of it is really spiritually neutral. The Bible lists examples of wealthy followers of God, like Abraham and King David, who were righteous in God's evaluation. Certainly Joseph of Arimathea, Luke the Physician and Lydia (Acts 16:40), the seller of expensive fabric whose home hosted a church, were wealthy believers. Scriptural examples of wealthy people who claim to follow God but live to worship material things are also prevalent. Read the parable of the rich fool in Luke 12:13-21.

Both righteous and unrighteous men and women have also come from the ranks of those whom God has chosen to give *less* of the world's wealth. The critical question seems to be, "What is the believer's attitude toward his material status?"

"But the one who is rich should take pride in his low position" (James 1:10). Again, "rich" indicates those who have more earthly possessions or power. The person whom God has given a great deal of honor and material wealth is in a position of greater responsibility to manage that status and those resources for the glory of God. Jesus said, "From everyone who has been given much, much will be demanded; and from the one who has been entrusted with much, much more will be asked" (Luke 12:48).

The "low position" of the person with more than his fellow believers is that of servant-to-all (Matthew 20:27-28; Mark 10:44). A Christian's position in life is not his own to do with as he pleases, but rather a trust from God to be used, managed and multiplied for His glory and the good of others. That is a humbling thought. To take pride in wealth that is given by God is to pretend that human effort produced it. But to humbly accept the role of a manager serving the interests of the kingdom of God with every resource He has given gives glory to our Heavenly Provider.[20]

Just as James assumed the role of a slave of Christ at the beginning of this chapter, in spite of his position as leader of the church in Jerusalem and half brother of the Lord, he now compels the reader who is wealthy in position or influence to assume an attitude of humble pride in his role of service to the kingdom. The deeper Christian life demands that the rich believer renounce all pride in his wealth and then take pride in his position of service to God. Real wealth is found in eternal things.

Take Pride in Eternal Possessions (1:10-11)

What incentives are there to adopt these attitudes which are so foreign to our human nature? Why would followers of Christ accept this new standard for their legitimate sources of pride in life? "Because he will pass away like a wild flower. For the sun rises with scorching heat and withers the plant; its blossom falls and its beauty is destroyed. In the same way, the rich man will fade away even while he goes about his business" (1:10-11). Our only real riches are those we possess in heaven; all else is but a fleeting privilege.

Wildflowers are a common sight in Palestine during their spring rainy season.[21] Anemone, cyclamen and lilies carpet the countryside with their brilliantly colored petals. The picture is one of breathtaking beauty and splendor. Just as commonly, the Middle Eastern sun comes in its intense heat to wither and brown the landscape that was briefly so gloriously attractive.

Every flower gardener can relate to this image. The blossom of the rose fades; with the cold touch of autumn frost the browned stems of the summer flowers are cut away to make room for a new garden in the spring. Impatiens wither and wash out in the direct light of the summer sun. Scripture frequently uses this image of fleeting beauty and the fragile life of a flower to describe our lives (see Psalm 90:5-6; 1 Peter 1:24).

Both the wealthy and the poor believer will pass from this life. At that moment material wealth is immaterial. "You can't take it with you" is a proverb taken from the truth of Scripture. Just as we entered the world empty handed, we will exit holding nothing of earth's honors or toys (see 1 Timothy 6:7; Ecclesiastes 5:15-16; Job 1:21).

But the wealthy have an extra temptation to forget that life is short. When the pull of possessions and high position in life is stronger than the pull of eternal values and the believer's position in Christ, he can find himself orbiting the wrong planet. As one man who had earned his first million dollars before his twenty-fifth birthday told me, "I don't own all these toys; they own me." The tendency to think only of this world, to value and take pride only in our earthly accomplishments is pervasive in affluent countries.

The look on African believers' faces when they sing about heaven is incredible to me. The obvious longing in their eyes for their eternal home with Christ is an image of conviction for those who honestly dread the thought of leaving this world. Those who feel that they have so much here that they are reluctant to leave it all miss the twin truths that life is short and heaven is the only place where we have any possessions worth living for. To forget this for even a day can cause those with so much of the world's temporary wealth to mismanage their resources and foolishly forget their added responsibility to the God who has supplied them for service.

Our mortality humbles all of us. The brown flowers of a sun-scorched desert are a yearly reminder that God provides the earthly blessings we find so attractive. Two points are poignantly made here: the wind and sun are swift and completely destructive to the flowers, and they are inevitable in their coming.[22] Christians must wisely trust in the Giver, take their values from Him and live for eternity.

Conclusion

What are you proud of? Take the place in which God has providentially placed you in this life as a source of pride in the love and wisdom of our perfect Father. Are you in humble circumstances? Hold up your head for the glory of God; don't waste time in envy of those with more. Rather than self-pity, exercise pride in the grace of God that has given you your position as a servant of the Lord of lords and the King of kings. Thank God every day for your rich, eternal inheritance in the Lord (Colossians 3:24).

Are you rich in talent or beauty or material success? Make your servant status your source of pride instead; God has entrusted more of the temporary things of His creation into your care. Humbly admit that these things are yours to manage and multiply for the kingdom of God for the short duration of this lifetime. Accept your added responsibility before God with the humble acknowledgment that you will need His grace and help to use these resources to bring others to know God's love in Christ. This life will end but our life in Him will not. Bring glory to God and give meaning to your life by your attitude toward the material blessings your Provider has given you.

The deeper Christian life is a life of giving, not hoarding. At the end of this century the average giving of an evangelical Christian for the work of God to reach a lost world amounts to only two percent of his income. In the United States, where more than 4 million households will go hungry every day,[23] those who are led by the Spirit of Christ must ask the Lord about our attitude toward being rich and poor.

If some have given all in the name of Christ, like John Wesley, George Mueller and Mother Teresa, leaving this world without a bank balance here, they left with an incredible balance in their heavenly accounts. Jesus said:

> Do not store up for yourselves treasures on earth, where moth and rust destroy, and where thieves break in and steal. But store up for yourselves treasures in heaven, where moth and rust do not destroy, and where thieves do not break in and steal. For where your treasure is, there your heart will be also. (Matthew 6:19-21)

Ask God, "Where is my life being invested: here or in heaven? What do I really value?"

Questions for Reflection or Discussion

1. Do you consider yourself poor or rich? Which does God consider you? How does your attitude about your financial status honor or dishonor God? In what system of value is every believer wealthy?
2. Does the command "ought to take pride" surprise you? In what sense is it righteous for a believer to express pride? Can you think of other verses that speak of "boasting" in the blessings of the Christian life? Does this give the believer license to feel superior to nonbelievers?
3. What is the "low position" of the person who is a materially wealthy Christian? What is the reason for humility in a person who has wealth and power but does not know Christ?
4. What does the person who is poor, powerless and oppressed have to look forward to? How can the truth of temporary material wealth help the wealthy believer keep his power in perspective? Where would that wealth best be invested?

Endnotes

1. J.D. Douglas, ed., *The New Bible Dictionary* (Grand Rapids: Eerdmans, 1962), 1333.
2. Martin, *James,* 17.
3. Mayor, *Epistle of James,* 349.
4. Davids, *Epistle of James,* 72.
5. Mayor, *Epistle of James,* 350.
6. Martin, *James,* 19.
7. Os Guinness and John Seel, *No God But God: Breaking with the Idols of Our Age* (Chicago: Moody Press, 1992), 32-33.
8. Adamson, *Epistle of James,* 60.
9. Ropes, *Saint James,* 143.

10. George Gallup, Jr., *Religion in America* (Princeton, NJ: PPRC, 1990), 21, 45.
11. Ropes, *Saint James,* 146.
12. Martin, *James*, 22-24.
13. Adamson, *Epistle of James,* 62.
14. Ibid., 62.
15. James Moo, *James,* Tyndale New Testament Commentary, Revised (Grand Rapids: Eerdmans, 1987), 67.
16. "Peter said to him, 'We have left all we had to follow you!'
" 'I tell you the truth,' Jesus said to them, 'no one who has left home or wife or brothers or parents or children for the sake of the kingdom of God will fail to receive many times as much in this age and, in the age to come, eternal life.' " (Luke 18:28-30).
17. Davids, *Epistle of James,* 77.
18. Martin, *James,* 25.
19. See Lesson 1, "Whom Does the Letter Address?"
20. Read Stanley Tam's *God Owns My Business* (Camp Hill, PA: Horizon Books, 1969) and Ronald Sider's *Rich Christians in an Age of Hunger* (Downers Grove, IL: InterVarsity, 1977) as excellent examples of this attitude toward biblical stewardship.
21. F.J.A. Hort, *The Epistle of St. James* (London, 1909), 15.
22. Martin, *James,* 27.
23. *TIME,* September 29, 1997, 23.

Lesson 3

James 1:12-18

Section A

Crowned Victorious over Temptation

James 1:12-15

Blessed is the man who perseveres under trial, because when he has stood the test, he will receive the crown of life that God has promised to those who love him.

When tempted, no one should say, "God is tempting me." For God cannot be tempted by evil, nor does he tempt anyone; but each one is tempted when, by his own evil desire, he is dragged away and enticed. Then, after desire has conceived, it gives birth to sin; and sin, when it is full-grown, gives birth to death.

The blame game is as old as mankind. Adam blamed Eve, and Eve blamed the serpent for their sin. Today, we like to blame our parents, the government, our spouses and one another for all our problems and failures.

Flip Wilson, a comedian in the 1960s, was fond of saying, "The devil made me do it." Occasionally men are so bold in their willingness to shift responsibility for their sins that they blame God. Pointing to where they were born or to their culture, they explain that God knew they would have these problems when He made them!

In this section of chapter 1, James follows the progression of sin from the initial idea in the form of a temptation to the act of sin and then the consequences. He emphasizes the truth that God has given the Christian a measure of control over his life, making it possible to overcome temptations. This section of James begins with a promise to those who win the battle with temptation.

Temptation Conquered (1:12)

This verse repeats the theme of verse 2, pointing the believer to maturity and completeness in Christ. The mature believer is persistently doing the right thing when tests and troubles temper his character. The specific arena of testing in this text is temptation to break the law of God—the temptation to sin.[1]

"Blessed" can be translated "happy, spiritually well."[2] The believer is happy not because he is tempted but because he is able to defeat his temptations. Without the power of God at work in the Christian through His Holy Spirit, the knowledge that we were breaking God's law and even the desire to change were absent:

> All of us also lived among them at one time, gratifying the cravings of our sinful nature and

> following its desires and thoughts. Like the rest, we were by nature objects of wrath. But because of his great love for us, God, who is rich in mercy, made us alive with Christ even when we were dead in transgressions—it is by grace you have been saved. (Ephesians 2:3-5)

As Romans 8 declares, believers are now free in the strength of the Holy Spirit to live according to the loving demands of a holy God.

The Christian who "perseveres under trial," who "has stood the test" is the happy, blessed one. The great assertion is that every believer can pass every test; success is possible! In an age of ready excuses and cultural rationalizations for every possible violation of the law comes the timely message that successful, conquering faith can pass any test and overcome any temptation.

We live in an age of victims. Even those who admit to committing murder blame their bad childhood, television, the stress of work and even caffeine for their crimes. The tendency to sue someone for every accident and to blame anyone but ourselves for our failures is rampant. The truth that Christ can enable any believer to defeat any temptation and to win spiritually over any test, says James, puts the control of our lives back in the hands of God.

As Paul promised the Corinthians, "No temptation has seized you except what is common to man. And God is faithful; he will not let you be tempted beyond what you can bear. But when you are tempted, he will also provide a way out so that you can stand up under it" (1 Corinthians 10:13). The person who stands up in

Christ to his temptation "will receive the crown of life that God has promised to those who love him" (James 1:12). James connects faith to faithfulness. This crown is the one reserved for victors, the *overcomers* mentioned in the book of Revelation.[3] The crown is the reward of eternal life, "promised to those who love him."

Love is defined by faithfulness to Christ. Jesus said, "Whoever has my commands and obeys them, he is the one who loves me. He who loves me will be loved by my Father, and I too will love him and show myself to him" (John 14:21). To the believer who, by grace and through faith in Christ, overcomes his temptations and persistently lives a holy life is promised a crown of life. This is the reward of the deeper life.

Temptation Conceived (1:13-14)

We now know the consequences of success, but why would anyone fail if failure is unnecessary? How does the sincere Christian end up on the wrong side of this promise? Understanding the problem of temptation can be an ally in the believer's battle against sin.

Where does temptation come from? "When tempted, no one should say, 'God is tempting me' " (1:13). The text begins first by eliminating impossible sources of temptation. God is not the source of temptation for two reasons:[4] *God is never tempted by evil,* and *God never tempts anyone to break His righteous law.* Those two important facts of theology are emphatically stated here. The moral testing that believers endure and their resulting temptations are not from God.

It is not that they were "testing themselves" but that they had "fallen into" (1:2, KJV) various kinds of trouble while living in a fallen world. Jewish believers during this period of church history were the targets of persecution. They should have understood that God "did not engineer their misery nor did He abandon them in it."[5] The test from God involved how they would respond to these troubles.

Men frequently blame God for their poor response to temptation and the resulting self-inflicted problems. Yet Proverbs 19:3 says, "A man's own folly ruins his life, yet his heart rages against the LORD." From the first history of the first sin of the first human, every person sought someone else to blame. Eve blamed the devil, and Adam blamed Eve for his choice to sin. It is not surprising that men eventually began to blame God for their sins in order to avoid personal responsibility. The hypothetical person speaking here who says, "God is tempting me" is incorrect.

When Jesus taught His disciples to pray, He led them to say, "And lead us not into temptation, but deliver us from the evil one" (Matthew 6:13). James is not concerned with teaching us the origin of evil, but with the practical understanding that our evil inclinations do not come from God. The Lord's Prayer, put in the positive, is saying, "Lead us away from temptation." All of us need this divine direction, the wisdom of James 1:5-8.

Where does temptation originate? "Each one is tempted when, by his own evil desire, he is dragged away and enticed" (1:14). The problem originates in us. Although our circumstances can make successful resistance to temptation more difficult, the human heart is the heart of the problem. "For out of the heart come evil thoughts, murder, adultery, sexual immorality, theft, false testimony, slander" (Matthew 15:19). When Christians take personal responsibility for their evil inclinations, they begin to defeat them. God is not tempting His children; believers are tempting themselves. As William Shakespeare wrote, "The fault, dear Brutus, is not in our stars, but in ourselves, that we are underlings" (*Julius Caesar:* I.ii.134).

What is temptation? The word used here also denoted the bait in a deadly trap.[6] This is not the trial or test but rather the enticement of sin. The purpose of bait is to attract the prey. Being led astray by our own desires is part of the irony of becoming trapped by sin. God has given us healthy, wholesome desires for things like love, achievement and survival. But when we seek to fulfill healthy desires outside God's revealed will, they become temptations to evil.

"By his own evil desire, he is dragged away and enticed" (James 1:14). Hooked, like a fish on an angler's line, we are reeled in, "dragged away," by our own misdirected desires. Following carnal lusts or indulging illicit fantasies is dangerous. Believers become trapped, hooked by them. The verb tense here indicates a continuous action; if we allow evil desires to control our lives we are continually "hooked" on them.

When Jesus Christ is no longer Lord (1:1), and our own evil desires become more important than pleasing God, we are the slaves of our sin. We are no longer living by the Spirit in a sanctified life and so we find ourselves "gratify[ing] the desires of the sinful nature" (Galatians 5:16).

Temptation's Consequences (1:15)

Sin has a life cycle, a natural progression from the moment it is conceived as a thought to the action and its consequences. James uses the metaphor of procreation to illustrate the development of sin as if it were a child growing up to have children of its own.[7] Sinful desire is personified as a forceful attacker. The birth of sin begins in violence, like a sexual assault. In the end, the victim is dragged away and enticed.

The focus of 1:15 is to describe the consequences of sin so that they can be avoided. Steps of prevention are suggested by the stages in the development of sin.

Resist

The easiest and best way to overcome temptation is to *resist it* before it becomes a plan and then an act. "An ounce of prevention is better than a pound of cure," says the folk proverb. Believers have a duty to resist temptation, to flee from it before it has the time to entrap us. "Then, after desire has conceived, it gives birth to sin" (1:15). If the unwary child of God waits until the sin has occurred, he has delayed action until it is too late to stand the test and succeed.

Repent

Thinking about a sin, toying with the idea long enough to entertain temptation, leads to acting upon our evil desires. But even after the desire has conceived and given birth to an act of sin in one's life, there is still a way to defeat the cycle of sin. Repent! Admit to God that you have sinned. Seek the forgiveness offered at Christ's cross. And make immediate plans to change your behavior and your way of thinking so that you will not repeat the sin.

The precious promise of First John 1:9 is, "If we confess our sins, he is faithful and just and will forgive us our sins and purify us from all unrighteousness."

The cycle of confession, forgiveness and cleansing can break the cycle of temptation and sin in our lives.

Or . . .

But what happens if we do not repent? "And sin, when it is full-grown, gives birth to death" (James 1:15). The consequence of sin is death. To continue to sin allows the power and domination of sin in the believer's life to grow until it is a deadly giant of monstrous proportions. "The wages of sin is death" (Romans 6:23).

The danger of allowing sin to control the life of the believer is real. Just as the promise to those who persevere under trial and stand the test of temptation is real, so the promise that sin produces death is real. The example of a Christian who sins and sins is a deadly example to those who do not share our faith in Christ. Being a "letter known and read" by other men (see 2 Corinthians 3:2), indicates that we are responsible for the results of our influence and example. Sin has deadly consequences that are just as eternal as those of faith and righteousness.

Conclusion

David Wells devoted a chapter in his book *No Place for Truth* to self-piety. He does not describe a life of personal holiness in which men and women strive to live Spirit-led lives. He *does* say that our current thought about sin and righteousness and judgment are not formed by the Bible's revelation of a holy God. Rather than dealing with sin as James does, the modern church is in danger of just renaming it and seeing it as a self-image problem.[8] When culture psychologizes life and does away with moral "rights and wrongs," we must acknowledge with James that both righteousness and sin have their respective rewards. One leads to a crown of life and the other to death.

Culture demands that we place the blame for our problems on God or our parents or our world. God's Word demands that we believers take personal responsibility for our sin and accept God's gracious offer of forgiveness and the strength to live a holy life.

Our opportunity is to live for Christ. Temptation is a fact of life in an evil world. Tests and trials of many kinds are inevitable. As fallen people, we will face temptation every day until the Lord returns or calls us into His presence. The message of these verses is that we can win. We can conquer temptation and do the right and holy thing. By God's grace in Christ, we are capable of wearing a victor's crown.

What is the secret to winning? Take responsibility for your temptations. Admit that your own evil desires are your real problem. Refuse to play the blame game. In James 4, we will discover that, in Christ, we can even defeat the devil himself. Stop flirting with temptation before you are dragged away and enticed by your evil desires. When you sin, repent immediately and ask God for the grace and strength to resist that temptation in the future. Refuse to allow a sin habit to take deadly control of your life. Conquer temptation in the name of Christ. Live by the Spirit of God active within you, and you can be victorious over your temptation. A holy life produces both present blessings and eternal rewards. May you wear the victor's crown of righteousness in Christ.

Questions for Reflection or Discussion

1. Does the idea that every temptation is defeatable surprise you? Does it seem to you that you sometimes are powerless to overcome temptation? Is "I can't help it" a truthful statement coming from a Christian?
2. How does the ministry of the Holy Spirit help the believer overcome temptation, persevere under trial and stand the test? Can you think of any verses from God's Word that promise the Holy Spirit's powerful assistance to allow believers to defeat temptation?
3. What is the reward of sin? What is the reward of success in being faithful to God? When does the believer receive the "crown of life . . . promised to those who love him"? Is there a sense in which he receives his reward now, or is this only a promise for the future?
4. Why do we tend to easily blame others for our moral failures? To whom do you most often ascribe blame for your sins? Why is blaming others self-defeating? Where is the real source of our failure to overcome temptation?
5. Does the image of an attack leading to the birth of sin, its growth into a deadly monster and the eventual death of its true parent seem graphic to you? Why would James use such a poignant literary device to make his point? How does that affect the idea of toying with temptation?
6. What are the steps to breaking the cycle of temptation, failure, sin and death? Are you encouraged by the promise that this cycle can be broken, leading to a victorious and holy life?

Section B

Redeemed by Consistent Grace

James 1:16-18

> *Don't be deceived, my dear brothers. Every good and perfect gift is from above, coming down from the Father of the heavenly lights, who does not change like shifting shadows. He chose to give us birth through the word of truth, that we might be a kind of firstfruits of all he created.*

If God is not the source of temptation, He is the source of good. The second half of this lesson takes James' readers to the opposite end of the spectrum of good and evil. The problems of living in a fallen world blinded by Satan (2 Corinthians 4:4) sometimes affect the thinking of a deceived church. Christians are likely to think erroneously that their problems come from God and their blessings come from their own efforts. We are even sometimes deceived about what is good and what is bad.

"Exercise . . . eat your spinach . . . take your medicine; it's good for you." The problem with many of the good things in life is that they do not seem so good to us. The result is that we do not always recognize good things. In *The Problem of Pain,* C.S. Lewis said:

> Any consideration of the goodness of God at once threatens us with the following dilemma.

> On the one hand, if God is wiser than we are, His judgment must differ from ours on many things, and not the least on good and evil. What seems to us good may therefore not be good in His eyes, and what seems to us evil may not be evil.[9]

Beginning with a necessary warning, this passage is the bridge from the truth that God never tempts us to sin to the truth of God's consistent grace to us. Unlike the fickle gods of the Greek pantheon who would either torture or heal their worshipers on a whim, the God of the Bible is constantly good in His relationship to us. Knowing this truth can transform our understanding of many life experiences.

God Is Gracious: The Source of Every Benefit (1:16-17)

We must be warned! "Don't be deceived, my dear brothers." James could be referring to the previous paragraph. There he warned that those who blame God for their temptations are wrong. The source of our temptations to evil is within us. Our own evil desires are the problem (1:14).

Satan is a deceiver (John 8:44) and one of the influences in the world who morally blinds those who give him a hearing. Christians bent upon rationalizing their actions regularly deceive themselves. Paul warned the Corinthians, "Do not deceive yourselves" (1 Corinthians 3:18).

We are prone to think God is not always good to us. We often think that the good things in life are the results of either our own work or a just reward for our own righteousness. One whole segment of Christians believes that we are "King's kids," deserving only the best and easiest that life has to offer. The warning in James 1:16 may refer to any of these deceptions.

"Every good and perfect gift is from above" (1:17). The nature of a gift is, by definition, something undeserved. Every gift of God from salvation to the smallest blessing of life is neither earned nor deserved. Many dear brothers are misinformed about this fact.

This grace, which is a gift from God, is being contrasted with the temptations and sins that do not come from God. While evil desires do come from us, every good gift comes from God, "from above." The greatest gift of all is eternal life in Christ. "He will receive the crown of life that God has promised to those who love him" (1:12). "For it is by grace you have been saved, through faith—and this is not from yourselves, it is the gift of God" (Ephesians 2:8).

Every blessing shouts the truth that God must receive all the credit for the good things in our lives. God wills to do good and only good for His people.[10] Rather than crediting our own luck, abilities or connections, Christians must gratefully acknowledge that God is the Source of our blessings, of "every good and perfect gift." Although James has been criticized for a lack of theology in his brief letter, this is a fundamental truth concerning the character of God. Into the soft ground of the worldview of his day, which included the idea that God might be tempting His people and that He might be the source of either good or bad experiences in life, James drove this theological stake.

James has already mentioned tests, trials of various

kinds, wisdom, perseverance and faith among the blessings God introduces into our lives. Each one is considered "good and perfect" by God.

The problem of sin is that we attempt to satisfy good desires outside the realm of God's provision. Some have tried to say that not all good things come to us from God, but that all God's gifts are good. But James is telling us that all the "perfect" gifts, completely good in the sight of God, must necessarily have God as their Source.[11]

God Is Changeless: The Security of Every Blessing (1:17)

What assurances do Christians have that God will not change in His attitude of grace toward us? With everything in our environment changing at an exponential pace and each generation racing to keep up with technology, the only constant in our daily world seems to be constant change.

But God Himself is changeless. As the text puts it, "The Father of the heavenly lights . . . does not change like shifting shadows" (1:17). The word for change in this passage is a word used for the alternating teeth on a saw blade or the constant change of the seasons.[12] Like the moving shadow of a sundial or the constant sweep of a clock's second hand, life changes constantly. But God is the one stable influence in a universe of change.

Even the things poets like to refer to as constants change. The mountains shift on tectonic plates. Stars burn themselves out and vanish or fall, shooting from their orbits in a burning arc across the night sky. The only consistently good, absolutely gracious influence in the universe is God.

A friend of mine was in Ethiopia during an earthquake. He knew that the buildings there were not well constructed, so when the ground began to shake, he ran outside. He described the insecure feeling of having the ground jumping up and down beneath his feet. In a panic, he grabbed another normally stable object, a tree. Before he could release his hold, the swaying tree hit him in the face several times. His potential source of stability and safety actually harmed him!

Christ is a constant, stable foundation for the benefit of the believer. "Jesus Christ is the same yesterday and today and forever" (Hebrews 13:8). All other sources of security and stability will ultimately fail us. To avoid being "double-minded" (James 1:8), unstable and tossed by every influence of a deceptive world, the saint of God trusts in Christ.

God's promise of grace in Christ is referred to in Hebrews 6:19 as an anchor of hope for those who have fled the storms of life. The rock upon which the believer's spiritual house is founded is the truth of Jesus Christ (Matthew 7:24-27). As A.B. Simpson wrote in his hymn "Yesterday, Today, Forever":

Oh, how sweet the glorious message
Simple faith may claim;
Yesterday, today, forever, Jesus is the same.
Still He loves to save the sinful
Heal the sick and lame,
Cheer the mourner, still the tempest—
Glory to His name![13]

If God does not change, what is He like? "God is light; in him there is no darkness at all" (1 John 1:5).

The reference to God as "the Father of the heavenly lights" includes the idea that He is the author and source of righteousness.[14] The sun, moon and stars are the most dependable things in the created universe. The concept that God created all these speaks of great power. But the metaphor of light as the symbol of righteousness takes the depth of the reference to a deeper level. That God is utterly, unchangeably righteous, holy and good is a fact upon which man can depend.

The contrast is striking between the created universe, called into existence by the desire of God, and the sinful human desires just mentioned in the chapter which lead to a world of sin and death. God's new creation of life in Christ is contrasted to man's destruction of life by sin.[15]

A parallel idea is that nothing can eclipse the good purposes of God.[16] "What, then, shall we say in response to this? If God is for us, who can be against us? He who did not spare his own Son, but gave him up for us all—how will he not also, along with him, graciously give us all things?" (Romans 8:31-32). No number of trials, temptations, testing or travesties in human experience alter the fact of God's consistent love for us.

How do we know that God gives us only good gifts? We know because nothing, no person or circumstance of life, can defeat His grace (Job 42:2, Matthew 19:26). God is love, and God is pure light. His every action is in line with His character. Because God is unchanging, we can hold to this foundational truth in the trials and tests and temptations of living. Whether tempted to doubt God's goodness or to give up in the face of difficulty, imagining that this is just fate, believers have this corrective truth to guide their understanding of the world God has created.[17]

God Is Creator: The Salvation of Every Believer (1:18)

What is God's consistent choice for us? "He chose to give us birth through the word of truth, that we might be a kind of firstfruits of all he created" (1:18). The emphatic use of the pronoun "He" tells us that God Himself is the Giver of salvation.[18] As John put it in his Gospel, "Yet to all who received him, to those who believed in his name, he gave the right to become the children of God—children born not of natural descent, nor of human decision or a husband's will, but born of God" (John 1:12-13).

The new birth is a gift of God's grace. Even our faith does not demand such a gracious response. God has chosen and chooses now to give new eternal life to those who believe in Him through Christ. The contrast is between God's will, which gives us new birth and salvation, and man's will, which is "double-minded . . . unstable" (James 1:8) and involves us in the cycle of sin James just described in verses 13-15.

New birth comes to believers "through the word of truth" (1:18). Salvation is found only in the message of Christ, the Living Word, and in His gospel.[19] The Word of God, whether it is being preached or read from the Bible, is the message of salvation. Without its introduction into our lives by the messengers God has sent, we could never hear the truth and believe (see Romans 10:14-15).

What is the final outcome of God's constant grace? "That we might be a kind of firstfruits of all he created" (James 1:18). The God who created the galaxies, solar systems and the starry universe above us has made those who believe in His Son the first and best offering of all creation. The firstfruits and best of the produce and the firstborn and perfect animals of the people of God were to be offered to Him in acknowledgment of God's provision of everything His people possessed (i.e., Deuteronomy 26:2; Numbers 3:13). Even the firstborn children of the nation of Israel were to be dedicated to God as holy and belonging to Him. Luke 2:21-24 tells of the presentation of Jesus Christ at the temple on the eighth day of His incarnation to keep this command of God.

God's intention is to set a people of faith apart from all the other people in the world as holy and uniquely belonging to Him. The life of every one of these people is to be dedicated to God from its very beginning in the new birth of salvation. Christians are to live a separated, holy life in Christ. The God who has given such rich inheritance to people who are so undeserving can be easily seen as a generous Father who gives only good gifts to all His children.

Conclusion

What kind of God do you believe in? Is He a God of pure goodness, the Source of every truly good thing in life? Is your God consistently loving and kind, with infinite wisdom, giving you only the best things at the best times in your life? If that is what you believe, then you are trusting the God revealed in the Bible.

Jesus Christ was God's *first* gift to you. The new birth and eternal life which follow immediately after you believe the word of truth are the gifts of God's grace; they result from accepting the gift of Christ's life sacrificed on the cross. Do you trust God? When you are tried and tested and tempted, do you still believe God is unchangingly gracious and loving?

Where are you looking for the good things of life? Are you looking only to God? Or are you perhaps looking to God and your human efforts outside His will? God's loving purpose for your life will never change, just as He will always be the same. Ask Him to accept your life, given in dedication to Him, set apart from the rest of humanity as holy and belonging to the Father, as the willing offering of a thankful child.

Questions for Reflection or Discussion

1. Where do most people believe the good in their lives comes from? How much credit for the good gifts of life belongs to God and how much to us?
2. Why do you think James warns his readers at this point about the danger of being deceived? Are we more deceived about this issue than others?
3. Does the unchanging nature of God make us more or less secure? How about if we are caught in the cycle of sin mentioned in James 1:13-15? How about if we are persevering in a trial (1:12)?
4. Are you ever tempted to doubt God's goodness toward you? If so, in what circumstances does this occur? Can you think of other passages of Scripture that speak of God's constant, loving attitude toward His people?
5. Being the "firstfruits" of the new creation of God

in Christ makes Christians highly honored and valued above all of God's other creations. How should this knowledge affect the way we live the deeper life for Christ?

Endnotes

1. Ropes, *Saint James,* 150.
2. Arndt and Gingrich, *A Greek-English Lexicon,* 487-488.
3. Adamson, *Epistle of James,* 67-68.
4. Mayor, *Epistle of James,* 50.
5. Martin, *James,* 35.
6. Davids, *Epistle of James,* 83-84.
7. Martin, *James,* 36.
8. David F. Wells, *No Place for Truth* (Grand Rapids: Eerdmans, 1993),137-177.
9. C. S. Lewis, *The Problem of Pain* (New York: MacMillan, 1962), 37.
10. Martin Dibelius, *James* (Philadelphia: Fortress Press, 1975), 103.
11. Adamson, *Epistle of James,* 74.
12. Ibid.
13. "Yesterday, Today, Forever," *Hymns of the Christian Life* (Harrisburg, PA: Christian Publications, 1978 ed.), 119.
14. Davids, *Epistle of James,* 87.
15. Martin, *James,* 39.
16. Adamson, *Epistle of James,* 75.
17. Martin, *James,* 39.
18. Adamson, *Epistle of James,* 75.
19. Davids, *Epistle of James,* 89.

Lesson 4

James 1:19-27

Section A

Characterized by Righteous Choices

James 1:19-21

My dear brothers, take note of this: Everyone should be quick to listen, slow to speak and slow to become angry, for man's anger does not bring about the righteous life that God desires. Therefore, get rid of all moral filth and the evil that is so prevalent and humbly accept the word planted in you, which can save you.

Selective memory is a term describing our tendency to remember what we want to remember and to forget everything else. We remember the times when we were sensitive and attentive while listening to our spouse or our child at a moment of particular need, but we forget all the times we were too busy to listen or just delivered our lines and left the stage. I personally like to remember all the times I have been patient when others were being difficult or circumstances were frustrating but prefer to erase the memory of those times when I have lost my temper and said or done things that I am ashamed of.

James helps us remember the aspects of our Christian lives that are in trouble, things which we would often like to forget. The point of the letter we are reading is to urge us to actually live "the righteous life that God desires" (1:20). The deeper Christian life can be described by this phrase. According to this section, it is a life characterized by righteous choices. As James calls upon fellow Christians to "take note of this" (1:19), all Christians must recall the choices we have made and attend to the life we are living for God. The word translated "therefore" here, sometimes translated "wherefore" (KJV), indicates that the new birth must now have some concrete results in the conduct of James' spiritual brothers.[1]

How we choose to live the Christian life is important to God. As A.W. Tozer put it:

> The truth received in power shifts the basis of life from Adam to Christ and a new set of motives goes to work within the soul. A new and different Spirit enters the personality and makes the believing man new in every department of his being. . . . With the ideas here expressed most Christians will agree, but the gulf between theory and practice is so great as to be terrifying.[2]

In the first part of this lesson, three righteous choices are outlined which can lead to the kind of holy life God desires for all of us. God can enable the believer to close the gap between theory and practice in the Christian life.

Choose to Listen More Than You Speak (1:19-20)

The moment we read, "Everyone should be quick to listen" (1:19), our minds jump to the name of some person who really ought to read and follow this injunction. But the verse begins with "everyone." Those who seem least inclined to listen are often people who think they already know everything they need to know. The person who sees himself as a leader, a teacher, an authority figure or an expert does not feel the need to listen. Listening is only for beginners in the minds of the self-assured spiritual leader.

God is saying that the mature Christian is the one who is quick to listen (1:19). The word "quick" could be translated "eager, swift" as it is in the King James Version. James may be referring particularly to being open to listen and apply the Word of God as it is read or taught, "the word planted in you, which can save you" (1:21).[3] But his injunction is just as true when applied to Christian relationships.

The fact is that the opposite of the verse actually applies more accurately to the way many Christians behave: Christians are often slow to listen, quick to speak and quick to become angry, thinking that their "righteous indignation" can bring about the righteous life that God demands. The first-century believer was in need of this imperative as much as those who followed Him in the faith.

The disciples once tried to force faith upon others and sought permission to call down fire from heaven when their attempts failed (Luke 9:52-55). Jesus rebuked this methodology. Believers sometimes try to demean and criticize others into living for Christ. Or we refuse to listen when others seek to instruct us, proudly insisting that we are correct.

"Slow to speak and slow to become angry" (James 1:19) completes the thought of being eager to listen. Silence is a virtue as long as it is sometimes interrupted with wise speech. But talking and getting angry are both "knee-jerk" reflexes for fallen people who are frustrated or frightened or fatigued. The habit of losing your temper and unleashing a flow of verbal anger is too common to need much illustration. Every reader can point to some instance within the past when he or someone near him has become angry and said things that should have been kept silent. Or we could remember when carelessly chosen words spoken all too quickly offended someone needlessly.

"A fool gives full vent to his anger, but a wise man keeps himself under control" (Proverbs 29:11). The book of Proverbs frequently describes the attributes of a fool as a person who talks a lot, listens little and becomes easily angered (see Proverbs 18:2; 17:28; 16:32; 12:16). But a wise man allows the Holy Spirit to control both his tongue and his temper. Nothing is more out of place than a Christian mother or father screaming about loving God or being like Jesus to a frightened child. A cover story for *Moody magazine* was titled, "Sinners in the Hands of Angry Christians."[4]

Why is that such a contradiction? "For man's anger does not bring about the righteous life that God desires" (James 1:20). Expressed anger aimed at other humans, who are created in the image of God, is counterproductive to the cause of Christ. The contrast here is between the righteous anger of God at sin and "man's anger."[5]

Anger is not listed in Galatians 5:22-26 as one of the fruits of the Holy Spirit. Human anger is not a product of righteousness, so it cannot produce righteousness.[6] But we often want to believe that our anger is righteous and can produce the kind of holy life God desires.

God's intention is to make us like Jesus Christ. How we live is important to God. He is either pleased or displeased with the choices we are making. God is pleased when we choose to speak less, listen more and become difficult to anger.

Choose to Leave Immorality Behind You (1:21)

James intends that these commands be acted upon immediately. "Therefore, get rid of all moral filth and the evil that is so prevalent" (1:21). He urgently longs for us to be free from choices that displease and offend the Lord.

"Get rid" is a strong phrase that was used to describe removing a garment.[7] Paul used the idea to refer to the rejection of sin and the decision to repent (Ephesians 4:22).

I was once climbing over a fence into a field where a friend and I had permission to pick some wild blackberries. As I tried to clear the top strand of wire, my jeans caught on the fence. I fell back-first into a recent deposit from what must have been a large cow. I wasted no time in removing the outer shirt I was wearing. My shirt was repulsive. Getting rid of that onerous shirt became an instant priority!

James is commanding us to remove the "moral filth

and the evil that is so prevalent." Using the strongest possible terms, the repugnance of our sin to God is described. The English language does not have a word with the strength of negative impact to translate "moral filth."[8] The word refers to actions that are completely evil and morally corrupt. He speaks of evil as being prevalent—the rule rather than the exception. If the writer was addressing the culture of the Roman world, these words would not be so disturbing. But he began by speaking to "my dear brothers," his brothers and sisters in Christ!

Many are disturbed by this indictment of the church. "How could he speak that way to us? Who does he think he's talking to?" In his book *The Body*, Charles Colson gives a description of the church of this age:

> Even secular observers have noted how this demand for "feel better" religion is affecting church life and practice. . . . "Unlike earlier religious revivals, the aim this time (apart from born-again traditionalists of all faiths) is support, not salvation, help rather than holiness, a circle of spiritual equals rather than an authoritative church or guide." . . . What many are looking for is a spiritual social club, an institution that offers convivial relationships but certainly does not influence how people live or what they believe.[9]

The problem is that Christians in every generation rationalize and redefine sin so that it is something else. Rather than seeing sin as "moral filth" and "prevalent evil," we see it as something much more acceptable.

The wife of a church leader discovers her husband's addiction to pornography. The entrepreneur advertising his "Christian business" is arrested for defrauding his insurance company. More than half of single adult people professing to know Christ also admit to being sexually active. The problem of sin in the church is not a new one!

In order to live a life that is pleasing to God, all sin must be seen as detestable and immediately removed, like my smelly shirt. Evil and sin must not be allowed to be prevalent in the body of Christ. We Christians must choose to repent and to leave our immorality behind us.

Choose to Live by the Word That Saves You (1:21)

The second half of 1:21 uses the common metaphor of a garden or a vineyard to illustrate what God is trying to accomplish in our lives: "and humbly accept the word planted in you, which can save you." God has planted His Word in the soil of our hearts. The parable of the sower from the teaching of Jesus in Matthew 13 addresses the same theme.

The heart must be the right kind of soil if the seed is to be able to take root, grow and produce the intended crop. Each spring, all the gardeners go out to plow and till in order to make the soil receptive to the seeds or plants they will carefully place in that soil. All the rocks and weeds must be removed from the garden if the seed is to find a soft place to send its roots without being stunted by the competing influence of weeds.

If James is saying that our hearts are God's garden, then God is cast as the farmer. The seed is "the word planted in you." This may refer to the gospel message, as Christ explained in Matthew 13:19, "When anyone hears the *message about the kingdom* . . ."[10] (emphasis added). That message must be humbly accepted by faith if the hearer is to experience salvation. The one who understands the truth of Christ's atoning death, believes that Christ is alive by the power of God and trusts Jesus Christ for forgiveness and eternal life will experience the salvation God intends when He plants that precious seed (Mark 4:14-20).

But beyond that truth lies the truth of the Christ who comes to live in the human heart at the moment of salvation (Ephesians 3:17-19). Jesus Christ Himself is the Word that God plants in the heart of every believer at the new birth James just mentioned in 1:18. Paul told the Colossians, "To them God has chosen to make known among the Gentiles the glorious riches of this mystery, which is Christ in you, the hope of glory" (Colossians 1:27).

Christ lives in us through His Holy Spirit so that our lives will produce a harvest of righteousness. On the personal level, that means the ability and desire to make righteous choices and to live the deeper life we were created in Christ to live. And on the interpersonal level, it means that our lives will produce a harvest of righteousness in the lives of those who will be saved through our witness.

"Humbly accept the word planted in you, which can save you" (James 1:21). Humble acceptance rules out argument, resistance or refusal of God's voice. The pride that makes us deaf to what we cannot personally explain or understand completely is set aside. The anger that would interfere with God's message of love, that tends to plow up the good seed with the weeds, is humbly submitted to God's control. The weeds of moral filth and sin must be thoroughly removed. Christ is in control, producing in us a harvest of life and righteousness.

Conclusion

The righteous life, the life of Christ in us, is the life God desires to produce. This is our salvation, our hope, our faith. To accept humbly the requirement of righteous choices is another step of faith.

Make some choices right now. Choose to listen more to God, to those who teach and preach God's Word to you and to one another. Choose to get rid of any sin, any prevalent evil, in your life. Stop making excuses for sin or pretending that it is acceptable in the life of a child of God.

Ask God to forgive you in Christ and to cleanse you from your sin. Seek the grace to repent and never repeat the actions and attitudes that so displease our loving God. Choose to live by the Word that saves you. Through your consistent life and testimony God can save others. Live "the righteous life that God desires" (1:20).

Questions for Reflection or Discussion

1. Why is it so difficult to listen without interrupting when others are talking? Is it more difficult to listen to the voice of God in Scripture? What are some good techniques that have helped you to be "eager to listen"?
2. Do you see spiritual leaders as people who talk more than they listen or who listen more than they

talk? How does that affect your own behavior? Can you think of any other passages of Scripture that indicate that "less is more" when talking is the subject?

3. Can you name a circumstance in which anger accomplishes something desirable from God's viewpoint? How can we learn to be more difficult to anger? What is really the source of our anger—circumstances or our reaction to them?
4. Why is our sin more repugnant to God than it is to us? Were you surprised when James accused the first-century church of "evil that is so prevalent"? Do you think the present-day church is better or worse in terms of living a pure, righteous life?
5. What are some obstacles to facing sin in the church? What does the New Testament say about accountability and discipline in the church? How can we help one another "get rid" of sin in our lives?
6. What is the difference between just hearing the Word and having "the word planted in you"? How does the parable of the sower in Matthew 13 help us understand the need for faith and obedience? What does it mean to "humbly accept the word"? What kind of harvest can we expect from a righteous life that pleases God? from a polluted, weed-filled life?

Section B

Instructed by Biblical Application

James 1:22-27

Do not merely listen to the word, and so deceive yourselves. Do what it says. Anyone who listens to the word but does not do what it says is like a man who looks at his face in a mirror and, after looking at himself, goes away and immediately forgets what he looks like. But the man who looks intently into the perfect law that gives freedom, and continues to do this, not forgetting what he has heard, but doing it—he will be blessed in what he does.

If anyone considers himself religious and yet does not keep a tight rein on his tongue, he deceives himself and his religion is worthless. Religion that God our Father accepts as pure and faultless is this: to look after orphans and widows in their distress and to keep oneself from being polluted by the world.

As we continue the lesson begun in James 1:19, we proceed further along the course of making righteous choices. Upon what grounds is the believer to understand how to live to please God? How can he avoid the self-deception (1:16) so prevalent in the church? Applied truth from the Bible, the Word of God, is the only objective standard for the life of the believer.[11]

A doctor tells his patient, "Lose weight, exercise, stop smoking, avoid fatty foods." So the patient goes home to sit on the sofa, eat potato chips and watch television. We worry about our health but fail to heed orders from our doctors and recommendations from nutritionists that could save our lives. We listen intently to good advice but then fail to apply it to our lives.

In a world filled with religious advice, what is really true? The general paralysis of many Christians in applying the truth to their lives may stem from confusion. This text can answer some questions we have about true Christianity. "Is this just more advice that I am free to take or leave? Should I just do what seems best to me, or does God expect that I do everything He says?"

What is "true religion" from God's viewpoint? God requires three things listed here by James as examples of true religion: righteous communication, acts of selfless love and behavior that is holy and good in His value system. All these can be learned by studying the Bible and allowing it to instruct our lives.

Listen to the Bible Until You Live It (1:22-24)

Hearing the Word is not the same as living it. The average Christian in the first century did not have a written Bible. In fact, most Christians probably could not even read. Their only access to the Word of God was through its public reading. "Do not merely listen to the word" (1:22). James assumes that his Christian readers—or listeners—are coming regularly to a place where the Bible is being read.[12] Listening to the Bible being read or reading it are not being discouraged here. But hearing the words of Scripture are not an end, but rather a means to an end.

Unfortunately, unlike James' readers, many Christians at the end of the twentieth century are not coming regularly to hear the Word being taught or read. We are not reading it ourselves on a daily basis. George Barna's research reports:

> Time spent in Bible reading and Bible study has remained constant—and at a minimal level—for the past seven years. . . . Studies show that we have become a nation of biblical illiterates, lacking knowledge of what is in the Bible and showing limited commitment to applying its truths to our daily behavior.[13]

Listening to the Word is to be commended as an excellent first step.

Readers were in the house church or the synagogue listening to the Word of God being preached (see Acts 2:42-46; 5:25; 16:40; 18:4). Three times James tells us that listening is not enough: "Do what it says" (James 1:22, 23). The Bible is not like one of those courses students can just audit without taking the tests. Scripture is a manual for living written by God and meant to be applied to daily behavior.

A recently published book by T. and J. Schultz has the title *Why Nobody Learns Much of Anything at Church: And How to Fix It.* Like James' readers, those who hear the Word being taught and preached often do not leave the building before doing the exact opposite of what they just heard. Hearing is good, but believing and living the truth is better. The repeated command to "do what it says" is in the present tense. It means we are to continuously keep doing what we hear. It must be our occupation.[14]

"Do not merely listen," says James (1:22). The trip to the doctor will not effect a cure if the patient never takes his medicine or follows his doctor's advice. Just listening to the Word may be better than not listening, but it is not more effective in producing a healthy Christian life. Think about all the things James has already told his readers to do: be joyful in the midst of life's tests, be persevering in faith, seek wisdom from God, be thankful for the position in life God has given us, listen more, talk less and rid our lives of evil.

The difficulty in applying biblical truth to daily living was already a problem in the first century. Those to whom James wrote felt satisfied with just knowing what God desired.

While sitting in a small-town emergency room, I saw a woman enter with pneumonia. She was obviously very ill. As a nurse filled a syringe with an antibiotic, a doctor came to tell her the patient had no medical insurance. She told the poor woman how much the injection would cost. The suffering woman managed to say, "I have no money," as she struggled to breathe. The nurse turned to shoot the contents of the syringe into the lab sink.

As sad as that story is, it is even more tragic when people hear the Word of God every week or every day and never take it into their hearts and lives. So much life-giving truth goes down the drain every time it is merely listened to without any life application. As James said in 1:21, the word must be "planted in you" if it is going to save you.

A proverb might help to illustrate the problem: "Like a man who looks at his face in a mirror . . . and immediately forgets what he looks like" (1:23-24). In the first century, bronze and copper mirrors were common. The point is not that the mirrors had poor clarity, but that the person looked and immediately forgot what he saw.[15] How many times do people leave the house after a visit to the mirror only to wonder if they combed their hair or put their lipstick on? Looking without seeing anything is a common experience.

The point of looking into the mirror of God's revealed Word is to find God's will and to do it. To immediately forget the sermon, the Bible lesson or our daily devotional reading and never apply it is both silly and dangerous. James' first point is: listen to the Bible until you live it.

Look in the Bible Until It Sets You Free (1:25)

What effect does living by the words of God in the Bible have in our lives? A deeper life experience with Christ. James contrasts the listener with the person who hears and then applies the truth to his life. "But the man who looks intently into the perfect law that gives freedom" (1:25) is set free. A common misconception is that the law of God puts restraints on our lives. The truth is that obedience to God's Word, to Christ's commands, actually sets us free. "To the Jews who had believed him, Jesus said, 'If you hold to my teaching, you are really my disciples. Then you will know the truth, and the truth will set you free' " (John 8:31-32). Free from what? Just two verses later, Jesus said, "Everyone who sins is a slave to sin" (8:34). Freedom is found only through obedience.

"The man who looks intently . . . and continues to do this . . ." (James 1:25). The emphasis once again is perseverance. The Christian life involves a focused attention to hearing and living out the life God commands. A brief weekly glance is not enough. Constant reading and listening to Christian programs and Christian literature is only effective if the listener is "not forgetting what he has heard, but doing it" (1:25).

The reward for this diligence in following Christ is not only freedom from sin and its deadly effects, for "he will be blessed in what he does" (1:25). God's blessing is linked to performance. The love of God is unconditional, but the blessing of a holy life in freedom from sin and guilt is reserved for the faithful. Blessing follows obedience just as discipline follows sin.[16] Joy, peace, a sense of God's favor and great effectiveness for God are the result of hearing and faithfully looking in the Bible until it sets us free.

Live the Bible Until Your Religion Pleases God (1:26-27)

"If anyone considers himself religious" (1:26), that is his self-image. But does God agree with this man? The question is not, "How do I see myself?" The focus of the Christian must be, "How does God see me? Is my religion pleasing to the Lord Jesus Christ?"

James gives some tests for the listener to administer to his own life to see how his religion measures up. The first test is righteous communication: "If anyone . . . does not keep a tight rein on his tongue, he deceives himself and his religion is worthless" (1:26). Immediately this last paragraph of the chapter and all the teaching in the rest of the book about the use of the tongue come to mind.

Do I talk too much? Is my communication sweet

and helpful only to be ruined by becoming bitter and harmful later? Are my words encouraging, building people up in faith, or destructive in their judgment, anger and gossip? Do I listen too little?

My tongue is to be under control, like a horse with a bit in his mouth and the rider in control, directing its course. If my speech is out of control, then my claims to being religious will do no good. My religion is worthless to God. As my friend Pastor Martin Berglund says, "A relationship with religion is not necessarily a relationship with Christ."

If the listener has passed that test, another suggested test of our faith is: "Religion that God our Father accepts as pure and faultless is this: to look after orphans and widows in their distress" (1:27). The widow and the orphan were representative of the poorest segment of society in the whole biblical era. Old Testament commands to care for those who are in need are plentiful (Deuteronomy 14:28-29; Isaiah 1:10-17; Jeremiah 5:27-28; Ezekiel 22:7). In the context of helping others with the most basic needs of life, our Lord taught, "whatever you did for one of the least of these brothers of mine, you did for me" (Matthew 25:40).

Commenting on this passage, Charles Colson said:

> In anticipation of our Master's return, Christians are to be committed to biblical obedience, which means working for justice and righteousness, serving as advocates for the needy and powerless who cannot speak for themselves. When we are faithful to the challenges of Matthew 25 or the prophetic exhortations of Amos,

> we cannot help but make a positive impact on society. . . . When the Church transcends the culture, it can transform culture.[17]

The Word is saying, "Help the helpless." Christ has commanded that His followers care for the spiritual and material needs of a suffering world. The implied question of James 1:27 is, "How does your Christianity compare to the standard of God for religion that is pure and faultless?"

One church took this idea to heart by going beyond their annual Christmas and Thanksgiving offerings for the poor of their community. They adopted families in poverty. The families they adopted received equal treatment with the church families all year long: at birthdays, when school clothes were purchased and when it was time to send the children to church-sponsored camps in the summer. Their practical love became a daily testimony to God's love and to the message of the gospel.

The final test of pure religion is perhaps the most difficult: "to keep oneself from being polluted by the world" (1:27). One of John Wesley's *52 Standard Sermons* was directed to the vast numbers of "semi-converted, almost Christian" people in the Church.[18] Contrast a life and a religion that is polluted by worldly influences, greed and self-indulgence (5:1-6) to a living relationship with Christ that is pure and holy. The Holy Spirit longs to transform completely the life and then the religion of every Christian so that the Father will accept our worship.

Conclusion

A river that is ninety percent clean and ten percent polluted is still a polluted river. Keeping your life from being polluted by worldly values, worldly ideas and ambitions and worldly actions takes constant effort.

For James the initial step is to admit that the stream of your life is polluted and to ask the Holy Spirit to enter and to do a massive cleanup operation. "May God himself, the God of peace, sanctify you through and through. May your whole spirit, soul and body be kept blameless at the coming of our Lord Jesus Christ. The one who calls you is faithful and he will do it" (1 Thessalonians 5:23-24). Once the life is clean, it is to be kept clean from all the moral filth that might enter to cloud its waters again.

The ability to obey this command lies in a complete surrender to the Spirit of our Lord. The alternative is also described in Paul's letter to the Thessalonians, "For God did not call us to be impure, but to live a holy life. Therefore, he who rejects this instruction does not reject man but God, who gives you his Holy Spirit" (4:7-8).

What is true religion that is accepted by God? It is listening to the Word of God intently, remembering what you hear and doing it. Look into the mirror of the commands of Christ and compare your ideas and your behavior to the example and teaching of our Lord until your obedience sets you free from sin and self-deception. Live the life of the Spirit until your religion goes beyond words to acts of selfless love and words of encouragement and hope that build others up in Christ.

What are you doing for "the least of these" for whom Christ gave His life? What selfless acts of love could you do in the name of Christ? God's Word is the medicine we need; take it by faith and apply it to your life.

Questions for Reflection or Discussion

1. Just after a passage about being eager to listen (1:19), James proceeds to tell us not to stop at just hearing the Word. Can you list some instances when you heard a sermon, attended a Bible study or felt strongly that a passage from your devotions was particularly applicable to your life? How did that change your behavior that week? Was the change temporary or permanent?
2. What percentage of what we hear in church do we put into practice? Why is it so easy to forget the things God is saying to us through the Bible? Can you make some suggestions for remembering to apply what you hear?
3. How many minutes do you spend reading the Bible each week? How many minutes reading the newspaper, magazines and watching television? What is the major reason for not "looking intently into the perfect law that gives freedom"? Do you agree with George Barna's research that says we are becoming "a nation of biblical illiterates"?
4. According to a George Gallup poll, more than eighty percent of people in the United States consider themselves "Christian"—they "consider themselves religious" (see 1:26). How does the "religion" of the average church member do when tested on the three criteria of redemptive communications, selfless acts of love to helpless people

and being unpolluted by the influence of the world? How does your church do on this test? What could you do to improve your grade?

Endnotes

1. Adamson, *Epistle of James,* 78.
2. A.W. Tozer, *The Pursuit of Man* (Camp Hill, PA: Christian Publications, 1950, 1978), 20-21.
3. Ropes, *Saint James,* 168.
4. Rob Reynolds, "Sinners in the Hands of Angry Christians," *Moody magazine,* November 1995, 12-19.
5. Thomas Manton, *James* Geneva Series Commentary (Carlisle, PA: Banner of Truth, 1988), 138.
6. Davids, *Epistle of James*, 92.
7. Ibid., 93-94.
8. Arndt and Gingrich, *Greek-English Lexicon,* 745.
9. Charles Colson, *The Body* (Dallas: Word Publishing, 1992), 42.
10. Martin, *James,* 48-49.
11. Edward J. Young, *Thy Word Is Truth* (Grand Rapids: Eerdmans, 1957) is an excellent work on this topic.
12. Ropes, *Saint James,* 175.
13. Barna, *The Frog in the Kettle,* 115-116.
14. Davids, *Epistle of James,* 96.
15. Adamson, *Epistle of James,* 83-84.
16. Hebrews 12:1-13 is a rather complete description of the relative discipline or blessing of the child of God in relation to producing a "harvest of righteousness" in his life.
17. Charles Colson, *Against the Night* (Ann Arbor, MI: Servant Publications, 1989), 137.
18. John Wesley, *52 Standard Sermons* (Salem, OH: Convention Book Store, 1967), 11.

Lesson 5

James 2:1-13

Section A

Distinguished by Equality for Believers

James 2:1-7

My brothers, as believers in our glorious Lord Jesus Christ, don't show favoritism. Suppose a man comes into your meeting wearing a gold ring and fine clothes, and a poor man in shabby clothes also comes in. If you show special attention to the man wearing fine clothes and say, "Here's a good seat for you," but say to the poor man, "You stand there" or "Sit on the floor by my feet," have you not discriminated among yourselves and become judges with evil thoughts?

Listen, my dear brothers: Has not God chosen those who are poor in the eyes of the world to be rich in faith and to inherit the kingdom he promised those who love him? But you have insulted the poor. Is it not the rich who are exploiting you? Are they not the ones who are dragging you into court? Are they not the ones who are slandering the noble name of him to whom you belong?

A 1950s situation comedy featured the Cleaver family. June Cleaver was the perfect television mother. (She even cleaned the house in makeup and high heels.) The Cleavers had two sons: Wally and Beaver. Wally was an easy son to love. He was responsible and compliant—never any problem to his mother. Beaver, however, was constantly in mischief, embarrassing his parents everywhere he went. But June Cleaver loved them both and treated them with equality in spite of the difficulty their differences brought into her life.

God loves all His children equally. In spite of external appearances of inequality in material wealth, talent, influence or beauty, God has no favorite children. The Lord did not love Lazarus more than the rich man or the rich man more than Lazarus (Luke 16:19-31). The command in this section of James to treat all people with the same respect and love is an imitation of the love of God. Notice the contrast in how believers treat strangers and how the world treats them.

Believers Give Equal Grace to All (2:1-4)

"My brothers, as believers . . ." (2:1) indicates immediately that faith has consequences in daily relationships. To worship God, a believer seeks to understand and follow the example of God. In Galatians 2:6, Paul revealed, "God does not judge by external appearance." The Heavenly Father is more concerned with what is in a person's heart than with what he is wearing, what is in his bank account or what is on his resume.

Remember that James identified himself simply as "a servant of God and of the Lord Jesus Christ"

(James 1:1) in spite of his position of authority and his relationship with the Lord.

God gives His grace equally to all; He "shows no partiality" (Deuteronomy 10:17). The believers addressed here must understand that God's love melts differences among men of faith who are now brothers in Christ. Paul taught the same principle: "For there is no difference between Jew and Gentile—the same Lord is Lord of all and richly blesses all who call on him" (Romans 10:12). Salvation is equally available to all races, economic classes and genders. Sinners who come in faith find equal treatment in spite of their earthly circumstances.

> This righteousness from God comes through faith in Jesus Christ to all who believe. There is no difference, for all have sinned and fall short of the glory of God, and are justified freely by his grace through the redemption that came by Christ Jesus. God presented him as a sacrifice of atonement, through faith in his blood. (Romans 3:22-25)

Just as June Cleaver loved her sons equally, our Lord has no favorite brothers. All men worthy of His death are worthy of His love and grace. "As believers in our glorious Lord Jesus Christ, don't show favoritism" (James 2:1). To disobey Christ is disbelief.

Prejudice against a group of people is evil, but showing favoritism *to* a group of people is also evil. If Mrs. Cleaver treated Wally better because he was her oldest son, that would be wrong. If she treated Beaver better because he was her baby, that would be equally wrong.

James used a kind of parable to illustrate. He draws a careful word-picture in 2:2-4. Although he could have used two different racial or ethnic groups or two different groups in terms of talent, physical beauty or education, James chose two different socioeconomic groups for his illustration. These are probably stylized individuals rather than a story of an actual event he witnessed.[1]

A rich man in expensive clothing and wearing a lot of valuable jewelry enters a church meeting. On the same occasion, a poor man wearing shabby, dirty clothing seeks to attend the same church service. The rich man is given a seat of honor and the poor man given either no seat at all or a place of humiliation.

I will never forget the welcome I received as a visitor attending the Main Street Baptist Church in Lexington, Kentucky with a friend. The church is large and mostly African-American in its makeup. The leaders of the church showed me, a white seminary student, the same courtesy they gave to the members of their own pastoral staff and to visiting pastors.

Although I remember feeling uncomfortable and insecure in the fact that I was not worthy of their kind treatment, that church body had me sit on the platform with their pastors during the service and greeted me in the same warm way they greeted their own leaders. From the pastoral staff to the people of the church, they showed no favoritism; all who served Christ were treated with equal love and respect, even those who were just preparing for service.

Not everyone is equal, really. Some have more money than others. While some enjoy the power of being in the majority, others must form a minority.

God has given different gifts in different proportions to His people. A few enjoy great intellect, power or talents, while others are unintelligent, weak and lacking any outstanding abilities. But to make judgments of another person's eternal worth based upon these external differences is evil.

"Have you not discriminated among yourselves and become judges with evil thoughts?" (2:4). God's judgment is based upon our faith in His Son, Jesus Christ. The emphasis of "brothers," used twice in these four verses, is that we are related to one another. We are equal in God's sight. With amazing clarity of purpose, a direct question is posed: "Have you discriminated among yourselves?" The question demands an answer.

If the answer is, "Yes, we have," then you have "become judges with evil thoughts." The Greek verb implies "facing both ways," meaning that these Christians were confessing complete obedience to Christ while they were defying and affronting Him with their discriminatory actions.[2] An honest "no" means that we are behaving as believers in Christ and brothers by giving equal grace to all.

Believers Give Honor Based on God's Standards (2:5-7)

While He loves all men equally, God does honor some people more than others. "Listen, my dear brothers: Has not God chosen those who are poor in the eyes of the world to be rich in faith and to inherit the kingdom he promised those who love him?" (2:5). In the first chapter of the letter, both rich and poor believers were equally instructed to take pride in their relative positions in life as having come from God

(1:9-10). If James is not saying that believers who are materially poor are always chosen to have a special blessing from God, what is he saying? Adamson writes: "James does not spiritualize or idealize poverty. Poverty does not guarantee either faith or final salvation."[3]

The Lord honored a different kind of poverty: "Blessed are the poor in spirit, for theirs is the kingdom of heaven" (Matthew 5:3). Whatever their material status, God honors those who are "rich in faith." People without faith who are economically disadvantaged are not honored by God. But the Father does honor those who are wealthy but have not sacrificed their faith for that wealth. Those whose riches come from spiritual wealth are poor in the eyes of a materialistic world but honored by God.

Eric Liddel, whose life was depicted in the film *Chariots of Fire*, gave up the privileges of his wealthy family and Olympic fame to become a missionary. The world considered him a fanatic; God considered him faithful.

In this world, people without power and money and beauty are constantly discriminated against. A pastor's son who happened to be dressed in tattered jeans and a faded T-shirt, hair uncombed, was admitted to an emergency room, bleeding profusely from a large cut. In spite of the insurance card in his wallet, he looked like a "nobody," a street person. He nearly died from blood loss while others with minor injuries were treated. Why? Perhaps because he looked as if he could not pay.

It is also true that people with power and money are favored, regardless of their "inside": the art world chose a national museum of art to honor a man whose obscene paintings of Christ are an affront to any person with even a vestige of morality. The world judges people's value by outward appearances and treats them according to that assessed value.

External riches or external poverty have little to do with God's economy. God is interested in eternal wealth and poverty. The Father has chosen those who are "poor in spirit" (Matthew 5:3) and "rich in faith" to "inherit the kingdom he promised those who love him" (James 2:5). This same kingdom is promised in 1:12 to the one "who perseveres under trial." Faith in Christ, humility of spirit and loving obedience to God are the riches of eternity. This is the currency of the kingdom of God. God honors those with this kind of wealth.

"But you have insulted the poor" (2:6). The church was using worldly standards and judging people's worth based upon economic and social criteria. Remember that God accepts the religion that takes care of widows and orphans (1:27). To treat those who have nothing as worth nothing is an insult to their Heavenly Father. It is just as wrong to have contempt for those who have a great deal of talent, power or earthly wealth but do not have a relationship with God through Christ. Reverse discrimination is still discrimination.

The Church was doing just the opposite of what God commands. They were honoring the very world systems that persecute and exploit the Church of Christ. "Is it not the rich who are exploiting you? Are they not the ones who are dragging you into court? Are they not the ones who are slandering the noble name of him to whom you belong?" (2:6-7).

The "haves" of the world of the first century were abusing the Christians. The persecution of the Church began almost immediately upon the death and resurrection of Christ. The properties of Christians in the Jerusalem area were seized. Christians were dragged into court, like Paul and Silas and Peter, and accused of being false prophets and troublemakers. Christ was maligned as a blasphemer, an insurrectionist and a traitor to the Jewish faith. The treatment of Stephen and Saul in Acts 7 and 9 is an example of the economic and physical persecution of the Church by the government and religious systems of their day.

But the people being persecuted were evidently envious and full of admiration for the physical power and wealth of their persecutors. They were dazzled by the worldly trappings of the very people who were normally their tormentors and detractors. Although secular philosophers and psychologists normally dismiss Christianity as a superstition, the church tends to give great honor and credibility to these disciplines. They are "rich in knowledge," we think. In spite of the amoral lifestyles of sports and media stars and their vocal opposition to God and the church, Christians still want to know all about them.

We honor the wrong people, says James. While we invest time reading *People magazine* and watching the latest celebrity interview, we don't have time for the young Christian full of questions or the child in need of nursery care. "You insult the poor" is the accusation of this church leader. Every Christian and every church must answer that charge with their choices. Whom do you honor? How do you spend your time? What is your value system for people?

Conclusion

Favoritism among the people of God is wrong. God gives equal grace to all. In order to be followers and disciples of Jesus Christ, we believers must give equal respect and love to every person who enters our sphere of influence. The ones dressed in fine clothing and the ones in shabby clothing must be treated with all the love and honor due God's children. To do otherwise is to become judges with evil thoughts. The ministry of the Church and the focus of God's people must not be on the externals of race and educational level and social standing. Our focus is the eternal relationship we have with all believers, all brothers in Christ. Our prejudices must be identified, confessed and renounced in Christ's name.

Believers give honor as God gives it. Honor those with persevering faith, with a humble spirit that acknowledges that every good gift of life is from God. Honor those who love God and will inherit the kingdom. Bless them with your compliments and your admiration. If you have insulted those who are poor in spirit or materially impoverished but who love God, repent. Stop honoring world systems, philosophies and superstars who persecute Christians and are openly antagonistic to Christ. Refuse to be silenced by the world's wisdom of what is "correct" and honor God's standards for holiness and righteousness.

Bill Hybels, pastor of Willow Creek Community Church in South Barrington, Illinois, and his coauthor Rob Wilkins said:

> Humility is important for another critical reason. The Pecking Order, at its very skeleton, is

> built on pride and prejudice, on the belief that some of us are better than others. Humility is the wisdom to know that each of us, in the eyes of God, is the same: deeply flawed, yet precious. . . . Christ's blood was shed for Jeffrey Dahmer, Adolf Hitler, Mother Teresa, and me and you.[4]

God loves all people equally. That is grace. God honors those who honor Him and value what is important to His kingdom. May He grant us the grace and humility to do the same.

Questions for Reflection or Discussion

1. In what ways does God treat all Christians equally? In what ways does He treat us all differently? Does more in terms of talent or material wealth mean that God loves me more? less?
2. What forms of prejudice are there in the world today? How do they affect the church? List some instances from church history. How do we discriminate wrongly (Matthew 7:1)? How do we discriminate rightly (7:16ff; 12:33)?
3. Why is it wrong to treat some people well and other people better? Are we permitted to discriminate for or against other believers? If so, based upon what?
4. Is it prejudiced to stay home from church to watch a "great teacher" on TV? Would you be disappointed if you needed prayer and "the wrong person" came from your church to pray for you? Are you more likely to listen to a plain-looking Christian singing or to a great-looking Christian singing?
5. How can we give more honor to those with faith?

How do we honor the people and systems that dishonor God? (i.e., What do you do on Super Bowl Sunday? when your morality is challenged by an authority figure from a university or a mental health professional?) Which earthly titles are a big deal at your church?

Section B

Judged by the Royal Law

James 2:8-13

If you really keep the royal law found in Scripture, "Love your neighbor as yourself," you are doing right. But if you show favoritism, you sin and are convicted by the law as lawbreakers. For whoever keeps the whole law and yet stumbles at just one point is guilty of breaking all of it. For he who said, "Do not commit adultery," also said, "Do not murder." If you do not commit adultery but do commit murder, you have become a lawbreaker.

Speak and act as those who are going to be judged by the law that gives freedom, because judgment without mercy will be shown to anyone who has not been merciful. Mercy triumphs over judgment!

The subject of prejudice and favoritism continues in the second half of this lesson with an appeal to the moral code of God revealed throughout the Bible. Just as rewards await those who display the grace of God equally to all, the judgment of God is the plight of those who are only good to some.

"Who is my neighbor?" When Jesus was asked that question, He gave a surprising answer. The truth about neighbors is that they can be the people you least expect to love. Often they are complete strangers. Occasionally they are people you would not normally like.

Brent and Susan Haggerty are missionaries in Burkina Faso, West Africa. One morning while Susan was working in the mission residence and her husband was working in the office, shots rang out nearby. A worker ran into the office to announce, "A man is shooting people outside our gate!" After some time, another volley of shots rang out, followed by silence. The gunman had been killed by police.

The couple was planning a trip to another part of the country that day. As they prepared to leave, friends asked them to take a sick woman with them to take her closer to medical help. So they all crammed themselves in the car for the hot, slow journey in the heat of sub-Sahara Africa.

At the other end of their difficult journey, the woman had been taken for help and business was done. The Haggertys were anticipating their return trip. But another request for a ride was waiting. An elder in their church sought a ride back to the mission station with them. The young man who had snapped under the pressures of his life and had been killed by the police was the elder's son. They knew him! On the ride home, they comforted their friend.

During that day, an ill woman, a grieving father and a hurting church member all became the "neighbors" of Brent and Susan Haggerty. Some of these people were strangers, but all of them had a need that God gave the missionaries an opportunity to meet.

Your neighbor is any person to whom God gives you the opportunity to love in some practical way.

"Love Your Neighbor As Yourself": The Law Kept (2:8)

"If you really keep the royal law found in Scripture,

'Love your neighbor as yourself' " (2:8) continues the theme of applying the truth of God's Word to the daily lives of believers. A question is implied: Are the readers really keeping the law of love? Or do they just *think* they are loving their neighbors? Continuing the theme of showing favoritism and prejudice, James draws a contrast between those who keep this commandment and those who break it.

Why is this "the royal law"? Two suggestions seem to warrant attention. The first possibility is that this law is royal because Christ, the King, gave it.[5] Love is the motivation, message and mission of Christ. The Lord emphasized love frequently. "In everything, do to others what you would have them do to you, for this sums up the Law and the Prophets" (Matthew 7:12). The Golden Rule (Luke 6:31) is another way of stating the command to "love your neighbor as yourself."

This could also be a royal law because it is sovereign, reigning over all other laws.[6] When Christ was asked, "Teacher, which is the greatest commandment in the Law?" Jesus replied:

> "Love the Lord your God with all your heart and with all your soul and with all your mind." This is the first and greatest commandment. And the second is like it: "Love your neighbor as yourself." All the Law and the Prophets hang on these two commandments. (Matthew 22:36- 40)

The relationship of the command of God to love your neighbor (Leviticus 19:18) to the rest of the Law of God is made clear in Christ's teaching. Love is the first and second commandment.

Love is the test of discipleship: "All men will know that you are my disciples, if you love one another" (John 13:35). Love is a proof of salvation: "Dear friends, let us love one another, for love comes from God. Everyone who loves has been born of God and knows God" (1 John 4:7). Love is the most enduring of the fruits of the Holy Spirit: "And now these three remain: faith, hope and love. But the greatest of these is love" (1 Corinthians 13:13).

Love is the chief characteristic of God: "God is love" (1 John 4:8). Worship, discipleship and sanctification flow from the love of God now resident in the lives of His people. As John Wesley said,

> It were well you should be thoroughly sensible of this, the heaven of heavens is love. There is nothing higher in religion; there is, in effect, nothing else; if you look for anything but more love, you are looking wide of the mark, you are getting out of the royal way.[7]

No wonder James stresses the actual, real-life keeping of this commandment!

"Love your neighbor as yourself" (James 2:8). This is not a plug for narcissism. Men naturally love themselves. The challenge is to care as much for the welfare of others as we do about our own. The call to put others' needs before our own is the heart of Christ's command. The Haggertys' trip to another city would have been much more pleasant without a desperately ill person as a passenger. Their trip home would have been easier without a grieving father to console.

The conditional statement lingers as a question, "If

you really keep the royal law found in Scripture, 'Love your neighbor as yourself,' you are doing right" (2:8). Am I really keeping the Law of Love? If I am not, how can I know?

"Love Yourself and Those You Like": The Law Broken (2:9-11)

Favoritism is a form of hatred. That seems like a strong statement until it is compared with the next section of James 2. "But if you show favoritism, you sin and are convicted by the law as lawbreakers" (2:9). Loving some people to the exclusion of others is sin. The person who does this breaks the royal law. The problems in the church of the first century are the same ones encountered by the Church in every generation.

To the Jewish readers of this letter, only fellow Jews were "neighbors." In spite of God's commands to be kind to strangers in their land, they had contempt for non-Jews. In fact, the Sadducees and Pharisees led two competing factions of Judaism, each considering the other inferior. Add to this the prejudices of rich against poor, of religious leaders against those who did not share their privileged knowledge of the Law and the hatred of the Jews for the occupying Roman army, and you find a culture with much tension.

One problem is that these kinds of prejudices are often so nearly universal in a culture that the people of God do not recognize them as wrong. In fact, they are institutionalized by religious people. Churches once thought that excluding people on the basis of race was actually good. Policies that give church members preferential treatment when the church has a need ensure that some will have better treatment than others.

A woman whose husband had left suddenly after taking all the money out of their bank accounts and canceling their credit cards came to her church for help. She told me they actually looked up her donation records on a computer and refused to help her and her two sons with grocery money. She had not given enough to the church during the past year to be eligible for aid!

James gives the picture in this passage of a courtroom with the reader as the accused and Christ as the Judge. Royal court is now in session. "If you show favoritism, you sin and are convicted by the law as lawbreakers" (2:9). If the Law of Love is not kept—ministering God's love to anyone whom we can help—without favoritism, we become lawbreakers. A lawbreaker is "a rebel who throws off the rule of God and stands under judgment."[8]

James 2:10 is one of those troubling verses in Scripture that keeps people up at night. "For whoever keeps the whole law and yet stumbles at just one point is guilty of breaking all of it" (2:10). Just as a person who breaks ten laws is a criminal, the person who breaks one law is also a criminal.

If the entire Law of God is summed up in this one commandment, breaking the one commandment to love is like breaking the whole Law. The problem is that we take some violations of God's law seriously and treat others lightly.[9] James gives two examples: adultery and murder.

"For he who said, 'Do not commit adultery,' also said, 'Do not murder.' If you do not commit adultery but do commit murder, you have become a lawbreaker" (2:11). The two words "murder" and "adultery" have more than one meaning in Scripture. The literal meaning of these violations of the Ten Commandments might have been James' intention. In that case, he is saying that one sin is not better or worse than another. If adultery was common in New Testament culture and largely overlooked, it was never overlooked by God. Murder was considered a serious crime. Both were punishable by death. But only the law regarding murder was regularly enforced by the government of the time.

Symbolically, adultery referred to God's people worshiping idols. Those who show favoritism to the rich show more regard for money than for the image of God in other human beings. To be spiritually in love with something other than God is spiritual adultery.

Murder is seen as harming the poor in Jeremiah 22:3. Calling your brother a name of contempt is considered murder in the eyes of Christ (Matthew 5:21-22).

It is significant that Jesus Christ was called a "friend of sinners." Our Lord loved sinners. He loved rich and poor sinners, talented and untalented sinners, sinners of all colors and sizes and ages. Jesus came to be a neighbor to both the "winners and losers" of the world. He has sent His church to do the same. Anything else requires the judge to declare the violator a lawbreaker.

"Love All by All You Say and Do": The Law Fulfilled (2:12-13)

James warns believers ("my dear brothers" [2:5]) that God takes this command seriously. "Speak and act as those who are going to be judged by the law that gives freedom" (2:12). The command is comprehensive: "Everything you say, and everything you do" is governed by the knowledge that the Law of Love will be applied to your life.[10] Just as the theme of righteous communication as a mark of righteousness is constant in James, so is the theme of living a sanctified life of Christlike love.

When Jesus answered the question "Who is my neighbor?" He gave us the parable of the Good Samaritan (Luke 10:25-37). The Jewish priest who passed without helping the battered man in the ditch was not his neighbor though they were both of the same race. The Levite was not his neighbor, even if he prayed a little prayer for the poor man as he hurried by.

Only the foreigner, the Samaritan stranger, who bandaged his wounds and paid for his recovery, saying to the innkeeper, "Take care of him," was a neighbor. We will not be judged for our good thoughts or fine intentions but for what we actually say and do to help others in need.

Christians will be judged by "the law that gives freedom" (James 2:12). This phrase was used in James 1:25 to refer to the Bible, the revealed will of God in Scripture. Jesus Christ interpreted that Law of God in the Sermon on the Mount ("You have heard that it was said. . . . But I tell you . . ." [Matthew 5]). The Lord went beyond the letter of the law to describe and demonstrate its fulfillment. Christians are commanded to fulfill the Law of God by living it as He intended.

Believers are not saved by their obedience to the law (Romans 3:20-22) but they *are* going to be judged by it. An answer will be given to the King for the words we have said and the things we have done or not done in regard to our neighbors. To obey the Law of Love gives freedom on the day of judgment: freedom from guilt and from God's displeasure. It sets men free in the present from selfishness and self-righteousness.

What we need is mercy! Every conscientious reader must have felt a pang of remorse for some missed opportunity to say a healing word or to lend a helping hand. "Judgment without mercy will be shown to anyone who has not been merciful. Mercy triumphs over judgment!" (James 2:13). Mercy is love expressed to the undeserving, powerless sinner. The closing promise of victory for the merciful echoes Christ's promise: "Blessed are the merciful, for they will be shown mercy" (Matthew 5:7).

Contrast that victory with the certain judgment that waits for those who are heartless and unloving to their needy neighbor. In the parable of the unmerciful servant (18:21-35), Jesus revealed God's intolerance of those who receive His mercy but refuse to extend that blessing to their fellowmen.

Mercy means forgiving those who do not deserve it and loving those who are only cruel in return. Mercy is being kind to those who have harmed you and showing respect for all men of all classes and races. Such mercy goes beyond mere obedience to the royal law and fulfills its intention. When we pray, as the Lord taught us, "Father, forgive us . . . as we forgive," the necessity of mercy for those who have done us harm and who owe us a debt of love is brought to mind. Every time we seek forgiving grace, we are minded to express it to other men and to avoid judgment.

Jesus Christ forgave those who put Him on the cross. Stephen repeated the prayer of his Lord, "Father, forgive them . . ." as he was stoned to death for his testimony. A Dani pastor I once met in Irian Jaya, Indonesia went to the village responsible for the massacre of his family to tell them of God's love in Christ. He went on to become the pastor of the church God raised up among his former enemies. "Mercy triumphs over judgment!" (James 2:13).

Conclusion

Three roadways lie before us like an interstate highway with two exit ramps. The world and much of the Church is on the main highway, where we love ourselves and a few selected people who love us. Jesus said there would be no reward for those who love only people who love them and are good in return. Even sinners do that much (Matthew 5:43-48).

The first exit ramp keeps the command to love your neighbor as yourself. When, in the course of life, we meet a person in need of help, take the time to love him for Christ. That is the example of our Lord. Without showing favoritism to some over others, we help our fellowmen for Christ. Such love can win the world to Christ.

The steep, less-traveled exit ramp is the way of mercy. Here the neighbor being loved is an enemy who lives to harm us, a person who has been a prodigal wasting all the precious riches of a Christian heritage or a person with no power to return perhaps even gratitude for our loving care. The poorest, meanest, most thankless people of the world can also be neighbors.

Merciful love is the highest way. Such a life of excellence and love triumphs over selfishness, lawlessness and judgment. The lives of thousands of God's servants who gave their lives to minister to the helpless or the imprisoned or the poor give testimony to the power of mercy and love. May God grant us the grace to live the Law of Love in everything we say and everything we do.

Questions for Reflection or Discussion

1. Whom do you consider to be your neighbors? Who are the people you most often personally help when you know of their need? What needs are you commonly aware of that you do not feel any responsibility to do or say something to meet? In what way do you help?
2. How can you be a neighbor to those who cut your hair, wait on your table in a restaurant, check your groceries at the store? What about the needs of others whom you would not meet in the course of life: those in the inner city, in rural settings, in mental hospitals, nursing homes, in areas of your city where they speak another language? How can a person or a church be a neighbor to these people?
3. How do you explain 2:10? Is murder worse than adultery? Is adultery worse than not loving your neighbor because he is poor or seems undeserving?
4. Are you surprised that Christians will be judged? Can you find other verses in Scripture to support this idea? On what basis will Christians be judged? What is at stake in this judgment?

5. Are there any people in your life who seem to be intent upon hurting you? Have you ever thought of them as neighbors to whom you should show mercy? Why is this the "law that gives freedom"? If "mercy triumphs over judgment," what is the prize that is won?

Endnotes

1. Davids, *Epistle of James,* 106.
2. C.L. Mitton, *The Epistle of St. James* (London: Eerdmans, 1966), 84.
3. Adamson, *Epistle of James,* 109.
4. Bill Hybels and Rob Wilkins, *Descending into Greatness* (Grand Rapids: Zondervan, 1993), 123.
5. Adamson, *Epistle of James,* 114.
6. Ibid.
7. John Wesley, *A Plain Account of Christian Perfection* (Kansas City: Beacon Hill Press, 1966), 99.
8. Mayor, *Epistle of James,* 91.
9. Davids, *Epistle of James,* 117.
10. Ibid., 118.

Lesson 6

James 2:14-3:12

Section A

Derived from Dynamic Faith

James 2:14-26

What good is it, my brothers, if a man claims to have faith but has no deeds? Can such faith save him? Suppose a brother or sister is without clothes and daily food. If one of you says to him, "Go, I wish you well; keep warm and well fed," but does nothing about his physical needs, what good is it? In the same way, faith by itself, if it is not accompanied by action, is dead.

But someone will say, "You have faith; I have deeds."

Show me your faith without deeds, and I will show you my faith by what I do. You believe that there is one God. Good! Even the demons believe that—and shudder.

You foolish man, do you want evidence that faith without deeds is useless? Was not our ancestor Abraham considered righteous for what he did when he of-

fered his son Isaac on the altar? You see that his faith and his actions were working together, and his faith was made complete by what he did. And the scripture was fulfilled that says, "Abraham believed God, and it was credited to him as righteousness," and he was called God's friend. You see that a person is justified by what he does and not by faith alone.

In the same way, was not even Rahab the prostitute considered righteous for what she did when she gave lodging to the spies and sent them off in a different direction? As the body without the spirit is dead, so faith without deeds is dead.

A man died in the middle of a church service, and an ambulance was called. The paramedics carried out three rows of parishioners before they found the dead man. Telling the dead from the living can sometimes be a confusing task!

Is your faith alive or dead? How do you know? If spiritual health is like physical health, there should be some test we could apply to determine if the patient is alive and well. For example, every visit to a doctor's office or an emergency room begins with a check of the patient's blood pressure. As the nurse tightens the cuff around the patient's arm (sometimes until his eyes bulge), she can observe the reassuring beat of his heart. The two numbers of his blood pressure also indicate something about his state of health.

God has a test for your faith. As James indicated in the beginning of this letter (1:2), tests are good. The two questions to be answered by this test are: Is your faith alive and dynamic or dead and useless? What is the state of health of your faith? By defining dynamic faith, the last part of this second chapter gives us a test we can apply.

Dead Faith Is Merely in the Mind (2:14-17)

"What good is it, my brothers, if a man claims to have faith but has no deeds? Can such faith save him?" (2:14). This critical question demands an answer. The stakes are the highest possible to man—eternal life. The man in question "claims to have faith." He professes that he believes in God and is following Jesus Christ. But just the profession of faith is not the test that indicates the existence of a living faith. James asks, "What good is it?" (2:14). The implication is that some kinds of professed faith may be no good at all. Their ability to bring the person to a saving relationship with Christ is doubtful.

Jesus promised, "Whoever believes in the Son has eternal life" (John 3:36). The promise is true. Real faith, true faith, in Jesus Christ is the access code to the grace of God in Christ. But not all claims of "faith" are genuine. Jesus also said:

> Not everyone who says to me, "Lord, Lord," will enter the kingdom of heaven, but only he who does the will of my Father who is in heaven. Many will say to me on that day, "Lord, Lord, did we not prophesy in your name, and in your name drive out demons and perform many miracles?" Then I will tell them plainly, "I never knew you. Away from me, you evildoers." (Matthew 7:21-23)

With the possibility of self-deception of this magnitude, the faith of the individual Christian must have some means of verification. With a parable, James develops the test.

"Suppose a brother or sister is without clothes and daily food. If one of you says to him, 'Go, I wish you well; keep warm and well fed,' but does nothing about his physical needs, what good is it?" (James 2:15-16). The kind of "love" that would leave a brother or sister Christian naked and shivering, suffering from hunger is no good at all! This shocking example of callousness and false sentiment for the hungry and hurting illustrates the ineffectiveness of faith that "has no deeds" (2:14).

While traveling on an interstate highway, I was passed by a car with an interesting bumper sticker. The message on the car's rear bumper declared, "I care." Did the driver's caring extend beyond his paper declaration? Just saying, "I care," really is little help to anyone. Caring goes well beyond words. The brother with such deep needs will starve and die from exposure while hearing the shallow well-wishes of his negligent family.

Faith without action is like love that never produces any real help for dying people. The battle for "the righteous life that God desires" (1:20) is being waged in this letter on two fronts. James, the pastor and leader of a real church in a real city, is faced with superficial religion in his church. People read the Word of God and forget to apply it to their lives (1:22). People do what is evil and blame their temptations on everyone but themselves (1:13-14). Now they claim to have faith but have no visible action in their lives that would proceed from faith.

"In the same way, faith by itself, if it is not accompanied by action, is dead" (2:17). Here action is the test of living, dynamic faith. Does this patient have any blood pressure or not? It is possible for the human heart to beat without actually pumping any life-sustaining blood to the body. Although the heart is beating wildly, nothing is actually accomplished; the patient is dying. Claiming to have faith without any fruit of righteousness or Christlike action is like this false heartbeat. Dead faith is merely in the mind and never affects the life of the person who professes it. Such faith is not good for anything; the patient who has it will die.

Dynamic Faith Makes Men Act (2:18-19)

Dynamic faith is active. It does things, righteous things like Jesus Christ did when He walked the dusty roads of Palestine. To prove this, James enters into an imaginary debate. "But someone will say, 'You have faith; I have deeds.' Show me your faith without deeds, and I will show you my faith by what I do" (2:18).

The person who is the opponent in the debate is essentially saying, "I don't need to do anything in order to have faith. Faith and deeds are separate issues and not necessary in any way to one another." He is like the long line of people who say, "I don't need to attend church or read the Bible or pray like you do; I can believe in God and not do any of the things you do." James will prove that this claim is false. Faith never exists in a void of loving, righteous action.

"I will show you my faith by what I do" (2:18). The connection between a living faith in Christ and not just action, but results, is well established in Jesus' teaching. "I am the vine; you are the branches. If a man remains in me and I in him, he will bear much fruit; apart from me you can do nothing" (John 15:5). The fruit of a holy life is evidence of vital faith. If there is no fruit, there is no root in Christ. Sterile faith is not faith.[1] Look at the following example.

"You believe that there is one God. Good! Even the demons believe that—and shudder" (James 2:19). This was the one-sentence statement of faith for the nation of Israel which the Jews recited twice every day (Deuteronomy 6:4).[2] As this was a representative statement of all that separated believers from a pagan, polytheistic or idolatrous world, James is underlining correct content in what the professed Christian believes. The emphasis of the statement, that the person believes this with all his heart, indicates his sincerity. In fact, James pronounces that this belief is good!

Then where is the problem with this faith? Demons are also correct in their belief that there is just one true God. As they indicated on the shores of a lake in Gadara, they recognize Jesus as the one Son of God (Matthew 8:29). Faith requires more than intellectual assent to truth in order to be living faith. Demons believe all the correct things with the full knowledge that judgment is certain. The very knowledge that could lead to salvation actually condemns them.

Dynamic, living faith is more than being correct in what you believe. Living faith is more than an intellectual exercise in good doctrine. Living faith produces a life of fruitful action for the kingdom of God. Impossible to hide, this faith shows a watching world that it exists by what it does.

Delivering Faith Moves Men to Obey God (2:20-24)

The debate now continues with a stinging statement of fact and two poignant examples of faith at work. The first is Abraham.

> You foolish man, do you want evidence that faith without deeds is useless? Was not our ancestor Abraham considered righteous for what he did when he offered his son Isaac on the altar? You see that his faith and his actions were working together, and his faith was made complete by what he did. And the scripture was fulfilled that says, "Abraham believed God, and it was credited to him as righteousness," and he was called God's friend. (James 2:20-23)

If faith without any act of obedience to God is useless, then faith that acts upon the word of God is effective. Faith without obedience is not yet faith. Incomplete, ineffective faith was common enough to warrant the strong warning of this passage. A person who wishes to debate this is "foolish," and his faith is useless to him.

He can debate, or he can imitate the faith of great men and women of God. Abraham went beyond intellectual assent to the fact that God could care for Isaac. Abraham did not say, "God, You know I love You; I don't need to made this sacrifice to prove it." He took his son and the wood and the knife to climb the mountain and offer his son to God as he was commanded (see Genesis 22). Abraham, the Father of Israel, went beyond claiming to believe and acted in obedience to God because he believed. "His faith and his actions were working together, and his faith was made complete by what he did" (James 2:22).

The possibility of an incomplete faith is real. But real faith is also possible: "Abram believed the LORD, and he credited it to him as righteousness" (Genesis 15:6). Abraham was called "God's friend" because of a life of righteous choices, a life of faith in action. When God tested his faith, it was found to be real.

The most controversial verse in the book of James is probably 2:24: "You see that a person is justified by what he does and not by faith alone." Martin Luther considered this a false statement and sought to deny the authority of the whole book because of this verse.[3] Others have considered this to be an absolute contradiction of Paul's insistence that ". . . it is by grace you have been saved, through faith—and this not from yourselves, it is the gift of God—not by works, so that no one can boast. For we are God's workmanship, created in Christ Jesus to do good works, which God prepared in advance for us to do" (Ephesians 2:8-10).[4]

Paul and James seem to disagree on this point. But when Ephesians 2:10, "For we are God's workmanship, created in Christ Jesus to do good works, which God prepared in advance for us to do," is considered with the preceding two verses, the combination emphasizes the two sides of the same truth.[5] Paul is saying that works of legalistic righteousness, without faith in Christ, can never save anyone from God's just judgment. James is saying that faith in Jesus Christ is not faith until it results in a life of obedience and holiness.

As Paul said, we are God's creation in Christ for the purpose of doing good works. James does not state that this is possible apart from the grace of God in

Christ. He insists that every good gift, including the new birth, comes from the Father as a result of persistent faith (see James 1:18). The fruit of the Spirit (Galatians 5:22-26) demands the presence of the Spirit who comes to the life of the believer through faith in Christ (see Romans 8:9-12; 1 Corinthians 3:16; 6:19; Ephesians 2:22).

Jesus taught that men will be judged according to what they have done (Matthew 7:21-23). Merely saying, "Lord, Lord" and professing to have a relationship with Christ is not sufficient for being declared righteous, justified and made right with God. Judgment is based on saving faith and on the life that faith produces.[6]

Another example of faith in action is added: "In the same way, was not even Rahab the prostitute considered righteous for what she did when she gave lodging to the spies and sent them off in a different direction? As the body without the spirit is dead, so faith without deeds is dead" (James 2:25-26). Unlike Abraham, whose life was considered to be exemplary, Rahab was a sinner. How could a prostitute be declared righteous by God?

By faith! Rahab put her own life and the lives of her family on the line when she protected God's representatives and identified with God's people rather than her own (Joshua 2:1; 6:17; Hebrews 11:31). Why, in a fortified city, well armed and with a trained army, would she side with the ex-slave refugees from Egypt? Only faith in an invisible God could explain such actions. Hebrews 11:31 tells us that this faith saved her life and the lives of those who trusted God with her.

The faith that delivers men from judgment and death is obedient faith. Faith that acts righteously in the face of trouble and temptation saves men. "As the body without the spirit is dead, so faith without deeds is dead" (James 2:26). This faith has characteristics: it is persevering (1:3; Matthew 10:22; 24:13; Mark 13:13) and is evidenced in acts of love (Matthew 25:31-46).

If your heart is pumping efficiently, the test will prove that you have blood pressure. Without blood pressure, the patient is dead. In the same way, righteous, obedient action is the heart of faith and "the righteous life that God desires" (James 1:20). Without it, the patient is dead. The very spirit of faith is the kind of active response of an Abraham or a Rahab, or even of Christ who was obedient even to death on a cross for us.

Conclusion

Is your faith alive or dead? To live the deeper life, you must first be truly alive in Christ. If you claim to have saving faith in Jesus Christ, who forgives your sins and gives you the gift of eternal life, does your life reflect that faith? What are you doing that is explainable only by your trust in Christ?

Dynamic living faith goes beyond mere intellectual belief in proper doctrine. That faith is dead and useless now and in the day of judgment. Living faith produces the fruit of the Holy Spirit because He is at work in the life of every real believer.[7] What good is your faith? Pass the test of faith today. Live "the righteous life that God desires" (1:20) through faith in Christ.

Questions for Reflection or Discussion

1. Why is the idea that faith without deeds is inadequate for salvation so disturbing? What is the difference between this idea and the false doctrine of being saved through our own works? (See Titus 3:4-5.)
2. How does James 2:14-26 relate to Jesus' teaching in John 15:2, which indicates that every branch that remains in Christ bears fruit and that fruitless branches are cut off from the vine? Why does a lack of righteous action always indicate a dead faith (James 2:17)?
3. What does "[Abraham's] faith was made complete by what he did" (2:22) mean? In what sense is faith without action incomplete? The righteousness that was "credited" to Abraham was a result of faith: "Abraham believed God" (2:23). How was he "justified by what he [did]" (see 2:24)?
4. When a believer experiences the new life, what visible changes might accompany his faith? How does the Holy Spirit change a person when He enters in (see Romans 8)?
5. If the demons have correct beliefs about God, why are they not saved? What is the difference between a correct theology and a living faith?
6. Much has been made of the apparent contradiction between the teaching of Paul—that salvation is by faith alone—and that of James—that faith without works is dead. How does Ephesians 2:8-10 relate to the idea that faith must be expressed in the life of the believer to really be faith? How does the teaching of Jesus about a fruitful Christian life (see Matthew 7:15) apply to this truth?

Section B

Tested by Spiritual Discipline

James 3:1-12

Not many of you should presume to be teachers, my brothers, because you know that we who teach will be judged more strictly. We all stumble in many ways. If anyone is never at fault in what he says, he is a perfect man, able to keep his whole body in check.

When we put bits into the mouths of horses to make them obey us, we can turn the whole animal. Or take ships as an example. Although they are so large and are driven by strong winds, they are steered by a very small rudder wherever the pilot wants to go. Likewise the tongue is a small part of the body, but it makes great boasts. Consider what a great forest is set on fire by a small spark. The tongue also is a fire, a world of evil among the parts of the body. It corrupts the whole person, sets the whole course of his life on fire, and is itself set on fire by hell.

All kinds of animals, birds, reptiles and creatures of the sea are being tamed and have been tamed by man, but no man can tame the tongue. It is a restless evil, full of deadly poison.

With the tongue we praise our Lord and Father, and with it we curse men, who have been made in God's likeness. Out of the same mouth come praise and cursing. My brothers, this should not be. Can both fresh water and salt water flow from the same spring?

My brothers, can a fig tree bear olives, or a grapevine bear figs? Neither can a salt spring produce fresh water.

As James zeroes in on the life that God desires for His holy people, he often returns to the subject of communication. The words spoken by God's people are an important indicator of Christian maturity or the lack of it. Here is another test of true faith. As blood pressure, heart rate and body temperature are the first tests a health professional checks to determine the physical condition of a patient, James first gives his readers a "communication test" to determine the level of spiritual discipline of his readers.

Who is spiritually mature? Our author has already taught us that faith in action produces spiritual maturity, the outflow of the life of Christ in men (2:14-26). The person who professes to live the deeper life with his mouth must reflect that level of maturity in all he says. The ability to control our tongues, to discipline our communications, to keep carnal words from passing our lips, is the test James applies here to maturity. Personal righteousness leads to the interpersonal expression of the life of Christ in the body, the Church.[8]

The Tongue Testifies to a Mature Life (3:1-2)

James addresses the exhortation "not many of you should presume to be teachers, my brothers" (3:1), to those who lead the church. In all the imagery which follows these verses, the "sum total of what men steered in those times" was used to illustrate that those who teach in the church are guiding it.[9] Taking a position of teaching the church must be considered carefully.

In the first century, religious teachers were respected rabbis with the power of influence over their listeners[10]—and many of Christ's strongest rebukes were reserved for them (Matthew 12:36-37; 23:1-3). In the Old Testament, Israel's teachers were the target of many rebukes: "Have you not seen false visions and uttered lying divinations when you say, 'The LORD declares,' though I have not spoken?" (Ezekiel 13:7).

Any person in the church making declarative statements about God, Christ, Scripture or the Christian life is impacted by this cautionary word. Many more people were evidently "presuming to be teachers" than God had called to that role of leadership (1 John 3:7; 2 Peter 2:1; 1 Timothy 6:3). "Not many of you" would imply that too many tend to assume this position in the church.[11]

The warning includes the promise of judgment: "because you know that we who teach will be judged more strictly" (James 3:1). Our Lord promised that every Christian will face God's judgment for every word he speaks (Matthew 12:36). James goes beyond this idea to state that the influence of one who presumes to teach the church of God makes him subject to a more severe judgment. The "teacher" is responsible for his own life and for his effect upon the lives of God's children. This fact makes his words even more open to God's scrutiny than the average believer's.[12] False teachers will not escape this judgment, as James emphatically declares.

Carnal motives, like power and prestige or even money, could possibly motivate people to act as teachers (see Acts 8:9-23; 2 Corinthians 2:17). James has just insisted that words indicating faith must be accompanied by appropriate action: "We all stumble in many ways. If anyone is never at fault in what he says, he is a perfect man, able to keep his whole body in check" (James 3:2). Here is the test of maturity that any who presume to speak for God must pass. James includes himself first as a teacher and now as a fallible man. The problem of spiritual failure is common to all (3:2), even those who lead the church through their teaching.

Perhaps the most common area of failure in the Christian life involves the tongue.[13] The statement here is a truism, a statement assumed to be true for the sake of argument.[14] A person who can control his mouth can control the rest of his whole person (3:2). That person is "a perfect man," a man who is mature, complete—but not sinless. James has just stated that "we all stumble in many ways" (3:2).

Knowing when just to be quiet is a holy virtue. The picture here is an analogy of keeping the tongue in check, overcoming the tendency of the mouth to stay open when it "were more profitably closed."[15] As a recent quote in a magazine said, "Minds are like TVs. When the screen is blank, turn off the sound." The rule is to be eager to listen and slow to speak (1:19).

The tongue will testify to a mature life, a life of completeness in Christ. Or it will indicate that the person's life is not yet in the Spirit's control. The tongue will disqualify many to be teachers; but it will indicate that a few who are called and mature may teach. Christ's words on the cross are a striking example. He had no word of accusation, defense or criticism. Our Lord spoke forgiveness, love for His mother, a prayer to the Father and pardon for those who put Him there.

The Tongue Is Seldom Tamed (3:3-8)

Four metaphorical examples of small things that have great power illustrate the power of the spoken word and its untamable nature. Horses, though much larger than humans, can be controlled with the use of a piece of metal put in their mouths to guide them (3:3). Palestine was full of Roman soldiers riding their horses and steering their chariots, and the nearby Mediterranean or even the Dead Sea was full of examples of vessels being steered with a rudder.[16]

Ships weighing tons can be turned under full sail, steered by a relatively small rudder (3:4). Like a space shuttle or an ocean liner being steered by a single pilot, this feat of engineering was impressive to the first-century mind. Just as the magnificent animal may be directed with relatively small force and the large vessel steered by one man, the church may be steered by one person speaking. "Likewise the tongue is a small part of the body, but it makes great boasts" (3:5).

In his commentary on this verse, Peter Davids says that the body here does not refer to the church.[17] But others observe that James is using the relative size of the tongue to show the large effect it is capable of producing on a large body, namely the Church.[18] The potential for destruction is the next theme of man's use of his tongue.

"Consider what a great forest is set on fire by a small spark. The tongue also is a fire, a world of evil among the parts of the body. It corrupts the whole person, sets the whole course of his life on fire, and is itself set on fire by hell" (3:5-6). The contrast here could not be more stark. A large forest can be destroyed by a small spark; the whole body can be made corrupt, unclean and defiled by the wrong words escaping the lips.

Jesus warned that it is what comes out of a man that makes him unclean to God (Mark 7:14-23). An otherwise righteous life can be negated with careless words. James is saying that the world is like a tinderbox, a dry forest in a drought, and the sinful words men speak in pride or anger, lust or accusation are like sparks igniting a conflagration that will consume both the speaker and his hearers.[19]

What is the source of this vast destructive force? "The tongue . . . is itself set on fire by hell" (James 3:6). ("Hell" in the original language is "Gehenna," the Valley of Hinnom, where Satan was traditionally thought to have fallen to earth and which was also thought to be the location of the final judgment of man.[20]) The destructive power of the tongue comes from the devil, and the life-giving power of the gospel comes from God (1:18). The tongue's great potential for good can become a vast potential for evil when it is misused. Who controls your tongue? Whose bit is in your mouth? Who is the pilot of your ship?

"All kinds of animals, birds, reptiles and creatures of the sea are being tamed and have been tamed by man, but no man can tame the tongue. It is a restless evil, full of deadly poison" (3:7-8). Men of James' day were quite proud of all the kinds of animals they were able to tame and train to serve or to amuse them.[21] Who could forget the first trained elephant or killer whale he ever saw performing for a trainer? The lions in the circus tent or the dancing bears in the markets of Russia make a word picture to illustrate James' amazement at the dominance of man over animal.

Contrast this ability to master beasts, birds and fish with man's complete inability to control something as small as his own tongue! "No man can tame the tongue" (3:8). Augustine pointed out in reference to this passage that only God can tame the human tongue—its owner can't![22]

"It is a restless evil, full of deadly poison" (3:8). This "restless evil" is unpredictable in its occurrence. What Christian has not been surprised at some time to hear words of bitter criticism or accusation or anger coming from the lips of some saint, teacher or church leader? The church of James' day was not living what they professed, and their outbreaks of evil words were the sign of their immaturity. The poison of their words had spread through the body of believers, delivering death rather than life.

Contrast this to the command of Paul: "Let your conversation be always full of grace, seasoned with salt, so that you may know how to answer everyone" (Colossians 4:6). The words of the believer are to bring grace and life, rather than poison and death to their listeners. But the tongue is seldom tamed, so the effect of Christians' words are sometimes redemptive and sometimes destructive.

The Tongue Tells of a Divided Heart (3:9-12)

> With the tongue we praise our Lord and Father, and with it we curse men, who have been made in God's likeness. Out of the same mouth come praise and cursing. My brothers, this should not be. Can both fresh water and salt water flow from the same spring? My brothers,

> can a fig tree bear olives, or a grapevine bear figs? Neither can a salt spring produce fresh water. (3:9-12)

Metaphors are abandoned as James applies the truth his letter conveys in 3:9-10. The tongue is as unstable as a man without faith (1:8); these are the verbalizations of a double-minded man. The highest use of the human gift of communication is to praise God. The lowest use of the tongue is to curse God, or in this case, man made in God's image.

Blessing, explained simply, is verbally wishing another well. Cursing is just its opposite. Jesus' words, "Whatever you did for one of the least of these brothers of mine, you did for me" (Matthew 25:40) also applies to the believer's communications.

The cursing of the created image of God in man eliminates the possibility that words of praise will then be accepted by God. One cannot wish God well while pronouncing harm on the people He has created in His image. Just as the same spring cannot produce fresh and salt water or the same tree produce figs and olives, the same mouth cannot make acceptable praise while it is out of control and speaking condemnation upon other men (James 2:8-12).

I will never forget the disappointment and disillusionment I experienced as a teenager when I first heard a man singing Christian music in a church service only to see him drunk and swearing at everyone in his presence only a few days later. The voice I had associated with some of the most precious hymns of the faith was now associated with hatred and vulgarity. As James observed, "My brothers, this should not be."

Conclusion

Jesus taught that whatever is in a man is what will come out of him (Matthew 15:11, 18). If he is full of God's Holy Spirit and life, then words of life and grace will be the constant blessing of his words. His tongue will consistently testify to his maturity in Christ. The deeper life in Christ is like a "spring of living water" flowing out to all whom it touches. Or, if the man is a carnal man, a double-minded, half-Christian man, his words will flow with blessing and cursing, life and death, sweet perfume and deadly poison. As Moo said in his commentary, a person's speech is a "barometer of spirituality."[23]

Too often the tongue testifies to a divided heart, which alternately produces good and bad fruit. The vast potential of our communication for good or for evil must be impressed upon all who would be teachers and upon all who are part of the body of Christ, the Church. God's just judgment awaits those who teach, and all who speak naming the Name above all other names.

But God's people will not tame their tongues through mere human effort or strength of character. May God grant His Church the grace of consistent, mature lives in Christ, that our words may flow with all the infinite life-giving power of God and never be given to the enemy for his destructive work.

Questions for Reflection or Discussion

1. How does a person know God has called him to be a teacher? How would we find out we are not called to teach? Is there a sense in which all Christians are called to fulfill a role of teacher?

2. Why is the tongue so difficult to control? What are the most common verbal sins? Share some tips that have helped you to break some verbal bad habits.
3. Why does James say, "No man can tame the tongue"? Have you given the bridle of your life to the Holy Spirit, to self or to Satan? How can Christ be put in the "driver's seat"?
4. Our words sometimes make us look like hypocrites. What should we do when our words betray a problem in our lives? To whom should we apologize? How can we make restitution?
5. Does having this problem mean that a person is not a believer? (Hint: James repeatedly refers to his readers as "brothers.") Where can we find hope that we will be victorious in our speech?

Endnotes

1. Arndt and Gingrich, *A Greek-English Lexicon,* 104.
2. Davids, *Epistle of James,* 125.
3. Manton, *James,* 261.
4. Also see Romans 3:28; Galatians 2:16.
5. Martin, *James*, 80-84.
6. Davids, *Epistle of James,* 128.
7. See Charles Colson's chapter "Equipping the Saints" (pp. 275-292) in *The Body* as an illustration of what faith can look like in the life of believers who are also discipled for the work of the ministry.
8. Martin, *James,* 103-104.
9. Davids, *Epistle of James,* 139.
10. Ibid., 136.
11. Mitton, *Epistle of James,* 188ff.
12. Adamson, *Epistle of James*, 141.
13. Ropes, *Saint James,* 228.

14. Martin, *James*, 109.
15. Moo, *James*, 120.
16. Craig S. Keener, *Bible Background Commentary* (Downers Grove, IL: InterVarsity Press, 1993), 697.
17. Davids, *Epistle James*, 139.
18. Martin, *James*, 110-111.
19. Moo, *James*, 125.
20. Gerhard Kittel and Gerhard Friedrich, eds., *Theological Dictionary of the New Testament* (TDNT) (Grand Rapids, MI: Eerdmans, 1964), vol. 2, 80 and vol. 1, 657-658.
21. Adamson, *Epistle of James*, 145.
22. Mayor, *Epistle of James*, 430.
23. Moo, *James*, 129.

Lesson 7

James 3:13-4:10

Section A

Directed by Heavenly Wisdom

James 3:13-18

Who is wise and understanding among you? Let him show it by his good life, by deeds done in the humility that comes from wisdom. But if you harbor bitter envy and selfish ambition in your hearts, do not boast about it or deny the truth. Such "wisdom" does not come down from heaven but is earthly, unspiritual, of the devil. For where you have envy and selfish ambition, there you find disorder and every evil practice.

But the wisdom that comes from heaven is first of all pure; then peace-loving, considerate, submissive, full of mercy and good fruit, impartial and sincere. Peacemakers who sow in peace raise a harvest of righteousness.

When the world is looking for wisdom, where does it look? In the 1960s, the Western world began to look to Eastern religions, to gurus and maharishis. Rock stars and movie moguls took pilgrimages to China and India; robed figures chanted in airports and begged for money.

Others began to go into dark-paneled offices where the walls boasted various degrees to have their behavior modified; their mantra was "I'm OK; you're OK." Thousands now rush to seminars to learn how to win friends and influence people, how to be a success or how to fix their love lives.

The shelves of burgeoning bookstores in countless malls overflow with popular wisdom from every direction: movie stars explain their metaphysical experiences, political and business superstars define their success and psychologists tell us how to raise well-adjusted children. Thousands call the number on the glowing screen to ask their psychic future.

Even the church has its moguls and gurus—they write the self-help titles atop the Christian best-seller list! We look to these men and women, their teaching tapes and slick titles for wisdom. But James has already reminded us (1:5) that wisdom comes from God. If we want it, we must first ask Him, the Giver of all good gifts. How will we know if we have wisdom? Like real faith and spiritual discipline, the presence of true wisdom can be detected through a test James has given us. Let's take the test and see how we score.

True Wisdom Is Revealed by a Good Life (3:13)

The contrast between true heavenly wisdom and

false worldly wisdom begins with a challenging question: "Who is wise and understanding among you?" (3:13). In the first-century use of the word, wisdom was the property of teachers and rabbis.[1] Understanding referred to "anyone claiming to have expert knowledge and esoteric understanding."[2]

The church had its share of self-appointed teachers (see 3:1) and self-proclaimed experts. A person who claims to be wise and understanding must meet the requirements of God. His wisdom must be in accord with heavenly wisdom and his understanding must be a gift from God's Holy Spirit. Paul indicated in First Corinthians 2:1-12 that "no one knows the thoughts of God except the Spirit of God" (2:11). Mere claims of understanding are not enough to gain the office of a teacher or to correct the leaders of the church. Words are not enough.

Wisdom, like faith, is revealed by action: "Let him show it by his good life" (James 3:13). The word for showing or demonstrating wisdom is in an emphatic imperative form. Evidently the only platform from which a person can speak as a man of wisdom is from a life of consistent godliness, a sanctified life. Consistent with a statement that true religion acts to help the helpless and to control the tongue (1:26-27) and a statement that faith is only genuine if it is revealed by a life of faith (2:24) is this insistence that wisdom must be active.

If wisdom is knowledge applied in a spiritual way to life's problems and opportunities, then its presence or absence can be observed when we face those tests and trials of 1:2. The replies of Jesus to the word games and traps of the Pharisees revealed wisdom in the midst of testing. The judgments of Solomon in situations like the one where two prostitutes each claimed the same child as her own (1 Kings 3:16-28) revealed that God had granted the wisdom Solomon prayed for. The decisions of James and the Jerusalem Council concerning the Gentile believers avoided offending believing Jews and affirmed Gentile converts to Christ (Acts 15). That is wisdom and understanding!

". . . by deeds done in the humility that comes from wisdom" (James 3:13). As Ropes has observed in his commentary, real wisdom is "wisdom that results not so much in what one thinks or says as in what one does . . . practical wisdom."[3] Just as humility is the fruit of the Holy Spirit and is also a virtue that Christ commended in the Sermon on the Mount, it is also an essential characteristic of true wisdom, revealed by a good and humble life.

Earthly Wisdom Reflects Satan's Influence (3:14-16)

James' focus shifts now from the life effects of true wisdom and understanding to the results of false wisdom. "But if you harbor bitter envy and selfish ambition in your hearts, do not boast about it or deny the truth. Such 'wisdom' does not come down from heaven" (3:14-15). The discourse now becomes personal: "If you have . . ." Some commentators have asserted here that the author was confronted by people in authority who had become James' rivals and had formed factions in the church.[4] Others believe that a splinter group had split from the church and was opposing James and the church leadership.[5]

Rather than a spirit of humility, there was a passion for rivalry, a "harsh zeal"[6] that had infected some of those claiming true wisdom. Too many churches over the centuries have been infected by this kind of "wisdom." Some in the addressed church bitterly envied those in authority or in positions of spiritual leadership.

In addition to this, there was "selfish ambition" in their ranks. People you know who have sought to take control of a church or a denomination out of a political lust for power and position will suffice to illustrate the point here. Many churches' histories are marred by the record of an angry leader or a disgruntled and ambitious pastor or layman who formed a group that emotionally and physically withdrew from the rest of the church to form an opposing force. The press attends church conferences and denominational meetings these days just to catch up on the political in-fighting!

"Do not boast about it or deny the truth. Such 'wisdom' does not come down from heaven but is earthly, unspiritual, of the devil. For where you have envy and selfish ambition, there you find disorder and every evil practice" (3:14-16). Those who harbor such deadly attitudes should not be boasting about how wise and understanding they are. To do so denies the truth; it is lying! The truth is that they are not only devoid of wisdom; they are unspiritual. The Holy Spirit leads God's people toward humility and unity (1 Corinthians 3), not toward fanaticism and factionalism.[7]

If this false kind of wisdom does not come from God, what is its source? In an ascending order of moral reprobation,[8] James indicates the worst possible sources of such actions: "earthly, unspiritual, of the devil" (James 3:15). Earthly wisdom is political and competitive. It is carnal rather than spiritual wisdom. Its ultimate source is the prince of this world, the devil. All this is coming from people who professed spiritual wisdom and understanding! They were using carnal weapons to win carnal victories.

If the results of true wisdom are a good life and deeds done in humility, what are the results of false wisdom? "For where you have envy and selfish ambition, there you find disorder and every evil practice" (3:16). Hell inspires division among Christians, confusion and immorality of every kind. "God is not a God of disorder but of peace" (1 Corinthians 14:33).

The church in Corinth is a good illustration of a church filled with factions, disorder and confusion about who its true leaders were. Corinth also had a preponderance of immorality among its members. Those who claimed greater wisdom stood in opposition to Paul and the true leaders of the church (see 2 Corinthians 10 and 11).

Paul reminded them, "For it is not the one who commends himself who is approved, but the one whom the Lord commends" (2 Corinthians 10:18). Like Aaron and Miriam, who sought to impose their own agenda on God by claiming equality with Moses, self-appointed leaders who claim superior wisdom will fail (Numbers 12).

Those who bring unity to the body, the peacemakers, are the ones who will be called the "sons of God" (Matthew 5:9). The fruit of their lives is consistent with the life of Christ, their Master. And the fruit of the lives of those whose father is the devil reveals their true master even if their lips claim to follow God's wisdom (1 John 3:10).

In his book *The Body*, Charles Colson devoted a chapter to unity within the church. Pointing to all the church splits, pastoral firings and interdenominational strife he said, "In view of all this, it is not difficult to understand the two most frequent reasons people give for avoiding church, 'All Christians are hypocrites,' and 'Christians are always fighting with each other.' "[9]

Heavenly Wisdom Reflects the Spirit's Influence (3:17-18)

Look at the ultimate fruit of a life directed by heavenly wisdom: "But the wisdom that comes from heaven is first of all pure; then peace-loving, considerate, submissive, full of mercy and good fruit, impartial and sincere" (3:17). The first and highest characteristic of heavenly wisdom is *purity.* Adamson in his commentary has said that purity is the key to all the qualities of wisdom.[10]

Purity can be understood in more than one way. To be pure means to be holy, sanctified, righteous, without sin. Purity of wisdom can also mean wisdom that is not tainted with worldly ideas, actions and attitudes; it is consistently living out the characteristics that follow in the list.[11] A similar idea is revealed in Second Peter 3:14: "So then, dear friends, since you are looking forward to this, make every effort to be found spotless, blameless and at peace with him."

A wise man or woman leads a pure, sanctified life. Wisdom that comes from heaven is also *peace-loving.* A peace-loving person is gentle, refusing to fight or argue even when under intentional provocation.[12] "For the kingdom of God is not a matter of eating and drinking, but of righteousness, peace and joy in the Holy Spirit" (Romans 14:17). The Prince of Peace, Jesus, did not answer His accusers and tormentors with a single word or any act of retaliation.

Wisdom is *considerate.* A considerate Christian puts the needs and desires of others first, before his personal needs and desires. Believing the best possible thing that the facts will allow about one another is considerate. Not holding our own opinions so strongly that others are forbidden to disagree with us is considerate. Refusing to demand justice when we have an opportunity to show grace and mercy is being considerate—and being like our Lord.[13]

Wisdom is *submissive.* This is not a popular word in our age, but it is a good word. It means "teachable, willing to be corrected, eager to follow . . . one who yields to persuasion."[14] This does not mean following blindly, but with a humble servant heart and an open mind. The willingness to be corrected by those in authority is in short supply in every generation. Submission is the result of wisdom. The theme of Proverbs 15 is that fools reject and hate correction, while wise people love and heed it.

Wisdom is *full of mercy and good fruit.* Remember that the religion that God accepts as pure is showing mercy to widows and orphans (James 1:27), giving the same honor to the poor as to the rich (2:5) and doing acts of selfless love for the helpless and hungry (2:16). Jesus Christ showed mercy to us; how can a wise, understanding follower do less for others? The life of a person who understands the life of Christ must be necessarily full of this kind of good fruit.

Have you ever wondered what motivated William Booth to found the Salvation Army or moved John Wesley to start all those orphanages and hospitals while trying to reach a lost world? Why would Albert Simpson leave a prestigious pulpit in New York to begin to reach immigrants and spend himself and all his resources to found a mission organization to reach those who had never heard of Christ? The answer is *mercy.* Those who know Christ, follow Christ and live for Christ do the kinds of things Christ would do for hurting people.

Wisdom is *impartial and sincere.* As James has already proven, being a prejudiced Christian who gives preferential treatment to any class of people is evil (2:3). Refusing to take sides in a dispute and remaining neutral and loving to both parties is the secret to being a peacemaker (Matthew 5:9). Sincerely caring for all men, and most of all for God, is the mark of wisdom doing its work in the fickle human heart.

What kind of people can claim to be wise? "Peacemakers who sow in peace raise a harvest of righteousness" (James 3:18). Note the contrast here: Those who claim wisdom but harbor envy and ambition lead the church into disunity and anarchy; but the truly wise produce a bumper crop of peace among the people of God. They bring others to peace with God. And they model and produce true righteousness, the kind that is humble and merciful rather than proud and judgmental. The fruit of their influence on the people of God is the test of true wisdom from God.

Facing those who would split the church and divide believers into warring camps, James praises the peacemakers as the truly righteous and wise. Who is wise and understanding among you? Their lives will tell us who they are.

Conclusion

As the world is looking for wisdom in all the wrong places, the Church must do better. National church conventions have recently seen the media gathering like vultures as churches annually battle over social issues and doctrinal positions. Camps of "liberals, conservatives, moderates and fundamentalists" gather on the right and left while the world watches in dismay.

Every group in the local church claims to be the one with the corner on wisdom, understanding and spirituality. But they may all be wrong, in spite of their well-held beliefs. Wisdom is not so much a matter of what we know as it is the way we live. The reason true wisdom is humble is that humility is the only sane response to a perfect and omniscient God. Mercy is reasonable when we consider how God's grace in Christ has affected us. Each leader and spokesman must ask what kind of wisdom he has.

Doctrinal purity is important, and leadership should go to the most qualified, gifted people available for the cause of Christ. But the things that are essential to God have to do with a holy life characterized by a harvest of righteousness and peace. If any life is producing division, disorder and evil among the people of God, that life is not inspired by heaven, but by hell. All claims to the contrary should cease; they deny the truth and boast about something shameful. May God grant us as Christians and as churches the wisdom to be peacemakers who live a good life in the Spirit's strength for the glory of Christ. May He give us the wisdom to know how important peace and righteousness are to our holy God.

Questions for Reflection or Discussion

1. Do we really value humility in the wise teacher? (How do we feel when a teacher answers with an honest "I'm not certain" or "I really do not know the answer to that question"?) Is it true that the more wise a person becomes, the more humble he becomes? How would this be revealed in his teaching?
2. Why do people—even Christians—follow "successful" people whose lives are not characterized by righteousness and peace? What does our culture say about this? What does James say?
3. Why does false wisdom in leaders inevitably lead to disorder and every evil practice? What are the excuses that are usually offered for these problems?
4. How does the list of virtues here compare with the fruit of the Spirit listed in Galatians 5? What are the similarities and differences in the two lists?
5. Can you point to a "harvest of righteousness" in your life or in the life of a particular church as the result of some truly wise leaders? In what sense was purity involved in the lives of those wise leaders?

Section B

Submitted to God

James 4:1-10

What causes fights and quarrels among you? Don't they come from your desires that battle within you? You want something but don't get it. You kill and covet, but you cannot have what you want. You quarrel and fight. You do not have, because you do not ask God. When you ask, you do not receive, because you ask with wrong motives, that you may spend what you get on your pleasures.

You adulterous people, don't you know that friendship with the world is hatred toward God? Anyone who chooses to be a friend of the world becomes an enemy of God. Or do you think Scripture says without reason that the spirit he caused to live in us envies intensely? But he gives us more grace. That is why Scripture says:

> *"God opposes the proud*
> *but gives grace to the humble."*

Submit yourselves, then, to God. Resist the devil, and he will flee from you. Come near to God and he will come near to you. Wash your hands, you sinners, and purify your hearts, you double-minded. Grieve, mourn and wail. Change your laughter to mourning and your joy to gloom. Humble yourselves before the Lord, and he will lift you up.

A mother returned home to what can only be described as a nightmare. She found her two sons beaten and bleeding. One room of the house was in shambles. Who had done this? Why?

As the story unfolded, the older brother owned a penny. The younger brother picked it up, and the older brother commanded the younger to give it to him. Being proud and tired of getting orders from his older brother, the younger one threw the penny under a bed. When the junior sibling refused to retrieve the coin, a fight broke out. The brothers themselves had done all the damage to one another and to the room.

Most of the things Christians fight and argue over are like the penny in the story. The older brother would say that he just demanded what was rightfully his. The younger brother would have insisted that he was fighting for freedom from unfair domination. The truth is that they were fighting to satisfy their own selfish, carnal desires.

James will again contrast two kinds of lives. Lives submitted to self-indulgence and to pleasing a fallen world's demands represent a choice that some professed believers have taken. A life submitted to God is the alternative that humble saints have followed. The two lives and their results are clearly delineated in this lesson. The theme from the first half of this lesson continues to show the true wisdom of the peacemaker in contrast to the earthly carnal "wisdom" which leads to the kinds of division listed below.

A Life Submitted to Self-Indulgence Leads to Strife (4:1-3)

Writing to a church locked in the throes of in-fighting

and characterized by "envy and selfish ambition . . . disorder and every evil practice" (3:16), James asks a critical question: "What causes fights and quarrels among you?" (4:1).

Many church attenders can recall arguments among believers that have lasted for months or years. One would think that these "defenders of the faith" were arguing for the cause of Christ and defending some high, holy ground. But unfortunately that is not the case. Members of the church were fighting and quarreling.[15] Their motives were not high, and their cause was not holy.

"Don't they come from your desires that battle within you? You want something but don't get it. You kill and covet, but you cannot have what you want. You quarrel and fight. You do not have because you do not ask God" (4:1-2). The carnal pride, greed and envious ambitions of those who demand their own way lead to the conflicts that erupt among believers. James has mentioned previously that we sin when we are "dragged away and enticed" by our own evil desires (1:14-15).

The internal strife of a double-minded person spills over into the relationships of the church. The "battle within" becomes fights and quarrels without. The word for "desires" can be translated "sinful passions"[16] and is the root for our English word "hedonism." Those characterized here would define themselves as believers and even as "wise and understanding" (3:13). But they demand their own way rather than God's way and use the most carnal of tactics to achieve their own goals: they fight, quarrel, kill and covet.

What does James mean by "kill"? Does he really

mean to suggest that professing Christians were actually taking one another's lives? Many have thought that this is a more metaphorical use of the word,[17] like Jesus' usage of murder in the Sermon on the Mount (Matthew 5:21-22). There Jesus taught that calling your brother a contemptuous name is like murder.

Given the existence of the zealots and others among the Jewish community who believed that armed resistance was the best solution to the Roman occupation of their land, others have taken the word literally, the taking of human life.[18] The Crusades, the Spanish Inquisition and numerous wars over religion are sad evidence that those claiming to follow Christ have sometimes left the way of peace and taken human lives. But these tactics will never achieve the goals or desires of those who use them.

"You do not have, because you do not ask God. When you ask, you do not receive, because you ask with the wrong motives, that you may spend what you get on your pleasures" (James 4:2-3). Prayer must not be merely an extension of a selfish heart set on its own gratification. Some attempts to move God with praise that is actually a weak form of flattery feign real worship, but the Father sees through the prayers of those who are really just seeking the success of their own agenda.

Others, believing they are doing the work of God but trusting in their own resources, do not even bother to ask God to grant their desires. They prefer to seek to obtain their goals through fighting and quarreling. As Davids has said, "Doubt is trusting in one's own . . . worldly intrigues rather than in God."[19]

God will not honor such prayers. The gifts being

sought are not to build Christ's kingdom or to help others but to satisfy the carnal desires of those who are praying. A life submitted to selfish desires and succumbed to worldly struggling to get satisfaction will result only in strife—in the life of the believer and in the church.

A Life Submitted to Pleasing the World Leads to Separation (4:4-6)

What began as a personal question has now become a personal rebuke. "You adulterous people, don't you know that friendship with the world is hatred toward God? Anyone who chooses to be a friend of the world becomes an enemy of God" (4:4). Friendship with the world amounts to spiritual adultery. The Church is portrayed as the bride of Christ in the New Testament. For example, Paul said of the Corinthian church, "I am jealous for you with a godly jealousy. I promised you to one husband, to Christ, so that I might present you as a pure virgin to him" (2 Corinthians 11:2).

Loving the world more than Christ is the worst kind of double-mindedness. To love success or power or our own objectives more than the Lord is more than an example of a poor idea of love; it is "hatred toward God." This makes the person an enemy to the very God he claims to follow. The world is the "whole system of humanity as organized without God"; and this "hatred" is any deliberate act that follows that system rather than the righteous plan of God which He has revealed in His Word.[20]

All of the seemingly inconceivable things done in God's name that are not from God illustrate the possibilities for this kind of self-deception. A man who came to an abortion clinic to murder the doctors and workers claimed he did this to protect unborn children. The chaplain of the U.S. Senate once reported that much of the mail government leaders received from evangelical Christians could be characterized as hate mail. Such combative, worldly methods, like man's anger (James 1:20), will never bring about "the righteous life that God desires."

God is taking personally these attacks upon other believers and upon those whom Christ died to save. "Or do you think Scripture says without reason that the spirit he caused to live in us envies intensely? But he gives us more grace. That is why Scripture says: 'God opposes the proud but gives grace to the humble' " (4:5-6).

There is little agreement about the reference to the "spirit he caused to live in us" as to whether it refers to the human spirit[21] or to the Holy Spirit of God.[22] If it is the spirit of lust for what man cannot have, like the interest of Adam and Eve in the one fruit they were forbidden to eat, then James is encouraging his readers to resist their fallen nature. If James is speaking of the Holy Spirit, He lives in us both to resist the selfish desires of the human heart and to jealously guard our pure devotion to God (see Romans 8:9).

The proud insistence that I do not need God to accomplish spiritual goals can be seen in a prayerless life of human effort to get what I want. G. Gordon Liddy, of Watergate fame, lived such a life. His favorite philosopher was Nietzsche, who believed that the human will to power was the highest possible goal of life. After giving his life to Christ, Liddy said, "The hardest thing I have to do every single day is try to decide what is God's will rather than what is my will."[23]

The result of human striving, worldly working apart from God, is separation from God. As Isaiah 1:24 declares, God will be quick to judge His enemies. He will "oppose the proud" (James 4:6). And who could win anything with God opposing him? But God will "[give] grace to the humble" (4:6). That is the result of a Holy Spirit-led life of humble dependence upon God. Grace is getting more than a man deserves from a God who owes him nothing. Such wisdom comes only from God (1:5).

A Life Submitted to God Leads to Celebration (4:7-10)

The verses in this section contain ten commands. Their theme is repentance and forgiveness leading to the restoration of a good relationship with God. "Submit yourselves, then, to God. Resist the devil, and he will flee from you. Come near to God and he will come near to you" (4:7-8). Humility leads to submission, a voluntary surrender of the human will to the direction of the Spirit of God. "I have been crucified with Christ and I no longer live, but Christ lives in me. The life I live in the body, I live by faith in the Son of God, who loved me and gave himself for me" (Galatians 2:20). The following imperatives are some part of what it means to die to selfish desires and destructive efforts at success and to live and walk in God's Holy Spirit.

"Resist the devil, and he will flee from you" (James 4:7). The kind of "wisdom" being followed when men fight and quarrel is from the devil (3:15). Like loving and having faith, resisting the devil is more than just saying some big, brave words of defiance. Refusing to take sides, to fight, to express angry words or to demand selfishly that the rest of the church and the world give you what you want is resisting the devil. Submitting to God is resisting the devil. Faced with a life being lived in the Spirit and a commitment to do the will of God, Satan will retreat, leaving the field of conflict to fight someplace he can have a chance of winning.

"Come near to God and he will come near to you. Wash your hands, you sinners, and purify your hearts, you double-minded" (4:8). Worship, complete love for and devotion to God, and a life of service (1:1) characterize the life James models for his church. The price of such closeness to God is "a radical repentance-conversion that orients the whole person to God."[24] The cleansing James refers to is an illustration from the life of the temple. The priests would wash their hands before serving in the temple (Psalm 24:4; 73:13). Symbolically that came to represent the cleansing of life from the acts of sin that were defiling it (Isaiah 1:16; Jeremiah 4:14).

The purification of the heart meant that the inner life of the one who came close to God must also be cleansed from thoughts and desires that are contrary to a holy life.[25] No more double lives can be tolerated if the readers are to draw near to God! Sanctification is a total-life experience. "May God himself, the God of peace, sanctify you through and through" (1 Thessalonians 5:23). Allowing the Holy Spirit to cleanse the believer inside and out is a command given in the aorist tense to enforce its urgency and "once-for-all" nature.

True repentance, in James' time and culture, was evidenced by an outpouring of tears and grief (Jeremiah 13:17). As Manton said, "Holy tears are the sponge of sin; a hard heart must be soaked, and a filthy heart must be washed in this water."[27] "Grieve, mourn and wail. Change your laughter to mourning and your joy to gloom" (James 4:9).

Christians are often laughing when they should be weeping. The problem with the church to whom James wrote, with its factions and divisions, its fights and quarrels, came with the acceptance of this disunity and strife as normal. Instead of repenting of their sins, they were going on with life as usual, thinking they were loving, filled with faith and wisdom and submitted to God. But they were none of these things. The time to repent in tears had come.

This command to turn their joy to mourning and gloom is not a justification for all the pessimistic and depressed Christians in the world. Joy is the normal expectation of life in Christ (see John 15:11; 1 Peter 1:8). But a life immersed in conflict and selfish ambition is not a life of joy; it is a life of sin that must be renounced. Laughter is foolish as long as a person is engaged in sin.

Like the other bookend at the conclusion of this list of commands, the imperative to humble themselves before the Lord balances and reflects the command in James 4:7 to submit themselves to God. Submission and humility are mirror images in the Christian life. "Humble yourselves before the Lord, and he will lift you up" (4:10).

Humility is the antidote to all the sins this passage seeks to correct. The fighting and arguments which result from selfish insistence upon personal satisfaction melt away in the light of a humble submission to the wise providence of God (1 Timothy 6:6-8). Humility seeks the will of God in prayer before setting out to get what the person wants by any means necessary. Rather than forming alliances with the world in order to coerce others into satisfying selfish desires, the humble Christian waits upon God and lives the life of a peacemaker (James 3:18).

Humbling ourselves before the Lord would require all the steps the other nine commands identify. The repentance demanded here would mean humble admission of sin, drawing near to God through the blood of Christ to seek forgiveness and a determined turning away from sin in the future.

What results could this kind of submission to God and humility before God produce? Mourning will turn to joy. Though He resists the proud who fight and argue to get their own way, God becomes the ally of those who express humility (Proverbs 3:34). As James put it, "Humble yourselves before the Lord, and he will lift you up" (4:10).

First Peter 5:6 repeats this promise: "Humble yourselves, therefore, under God's mighty hand, that he may lift you up in due time." Our Lord promised that "he who humbles himself will be exalted" (Luke 18:14). Jesus Christ will one day turn his tears to laughter and transform his mourning into joy (Isaiah 61:1-3). Submission to God results, ultimately, in celebration with God.

Conclusion

Is your life a life of peace, or is it a life of conflict? Are you "fighting for pennies" of power and prestige and personal determination as you beat your brothers and sisters up with words and perhaps even actions?

No matter how noble your personal desires may seem to you, they are tainted by sin. Carnal, selfish motivations and contentious actions separate us from God, making us act like His enemies. They reveal that we are really in love with the world, giving the echo to its methods and motivations as we seek to satisfy our own desires.

The Holy Spirit of God within the life of every Christian jealously guards our devotion to the Father and to His desires. You and I can choose: God can either be our Adversary, resisting everything we seek to do by our sinful striving, or He can be a God of grace, multiplying our prayers and our efforts to do His will. We can proudly insist upon our own way—only to discover that we will always fail in the end to achieve it and be humbled by our broken dreams. *Or* we can humble ourselves to seek God's priorities and discover that He will exalt us with His Son.

These ten verses are actually a call to repentance. They indict the church that is locked in conflict, actually allowing the devil's wisdom and methods to control their lives. The cleansing power of the Holy Spirit is necessary in every area of the life in order to correct this problem. Churches that cannot have a congregational meeting without accusations, insinuations about the character of its members or leaders and the spectacle of red faces and raised voices need to repent.

The picketers and petitioners who protest the world's abuses must be certain that their spirit is the same as that of the Lord who loves and died for sinners.

The deeper life is a life of peace, seeking the cause of Christ in the Spirit of Christ. Worldly strategies will never succeed in spiritual struggles. God will bless and exalt the repentant, submissive, humble believer. May every Christian, every local church and every denomination follow the way of submission to God.

Questions for Reflection or Discussion

1. Why do Christians have arguments, bitter feelings and conflicts? What is the most common cause of hurt feelings and bruised believers in your fellowship?
2. How does James make the connection between losing our grip on grace in interpersonal relationships and trusting God in prayer to meet our needs (4:2-3)? Will God bless carnal tactics if the desired goal is good?
3. Read First John 1:5-7 and 2:7-12 where John talks about how essential fellowship with brothers and sisters is to fellowship with God. Now compare these passages with James 4:4-6. Is there ever a biblical reason to argue or hold a grudge against another believer? Why or why not?
4. How can submission to God solve the problem of wanting what we don't have? What is the connection with "resisting the devil" (see 4:7)? What are some other biblical references to resisting the devil? How does the Holy Spirit aid in this battle?
5. How can Christlike humility solve the problem of quarreling among Christians? How does humility fit in with submission to God? Do you need to repent of your behavior or attitude in any relationships? In your church's relationships with other churches or the community?

Endnotes

1. Kittel, *Theological Dictionary of the New Testament (TDNT)*, vol. 6, 962-963.
2. Martin, *James*, 128.
3. Ropes, *Saint James*, 244.
4. Davids, *Epistle of James*, 151.
5. Kittel, *TDNT*, vol. 2, 660-661.
6. Ropes, *Saint James*, 245.
7. Moo, *James*, 132-133.
8. Martin, *James*, 125.
9. Colson, *The Body*, 101.
10. Adamson, *Epistle of James*, 154.
11. Davids, *Epistle of James*, 154.
12. Ibid.
13. Manton, *James*, 318.
14. Adamson, *Epistle of James*, 155.
15. Ropes, *Saint James*, 253.
16. Martin, *James*, 145.
17. Mitton, *The Epistle of St. James*, 148-149.
18. Martin, *James*, 151.
19. Davids, *Epistle of James*, 159.
20. Adamson, *Epistle of James*, 161.
21. Davids, *Epistle of James*, 163.
22. Martin, *James*, 151.
23. Colson, *Against the Night*, 144-146.
24. Martin, *James*, 154.
25. Adamson, *Epistle of James*, 148-149.
26. Manton, *James*, 373.

Lesson 8

James 4:11-17

Section A

Humbled by God's Right to Judge

James 4:11-12

Brothers, do not slander one another. Anyone who speaks against his brother or judges him speaks against the law and judges it. When you judge the law, you are not keeping it, but sitting in judgment on it. There is only one Lawgiver and Judge, the one who is able to save and destroy. But you—who are you to judge your neighbor?

A friend of mine is a public figure, a man appointed to an important political position. I was shocked to read front-page allegations against him in my morning paper. If the charges made by another expert in his field were true, my friend was incompetent and negligent in his duty. I began to pray for my friend. When we were able to get together to talk, I discovered that the allegations were completely false, as was most of the information in the paper concerning the details of the incident in question.

My friend is also a committed Christian. He told me that he was choosing to allow God to defend him. He declined all interviews with the newspapers or television news to defend his name. He refused to allow the media to spread the circle of accusations and counter-accusations. The person who had set out to publicly destroy him was a man he had been forced to dismiss earlier in his career.

But not one word of criticism came from my friend against this man who was trying to do such damage. In the end, written in a back section of the newspaper was the admission that the charges were all proven to be false. My friend's name was cleared with the agency that was responsible to review the case to see if any misconduct had occurred.

Refusing to judge or criticize your brothers in Christ is difficult. Refusing to judge and criticize those who seek to destroy you seems impossible, but that is the command of this section. In a church divided by quarreling (4:1), the author now addresses the use of the tongue in the spread of such disunity and strife. The imperative is directed to the treatment of believers, but is equally applicable to all men.

Criticizing Your Brothers Makes You a Judge (4:11)

The command that forms the beginning of this verse seems couched in legal terms: "Brothers, do not slander one another. Anyone who speaks against his brother or judges him speaks against the law and judges it" (4:11). According to an attorney I know, slander involves making statements of a negative nature about the character or conduct of another person that can be proven to be false. In the case of those in the public eye, like politicians and pastors, the person making the statements must also be guilty of having a malicious intent in his statements in order to be guilty of slander. But our current legal standards and God's standards often differ.

Slander, in the biblical usage of the word, means "to speak ill of."[1] It is any kind of "unkind talk or harsh criticism."[2] By this standard, and unlike the modern legal use of the word, the negative statements can be completely true and *still* be slanderous. The kind of talk that speculates about another person's character or tells of another person's failures is slander. The King James Version translates this, "Speak not evil one of another."

This idea is supported by Old and New Testament usages.[3] "You speak continually against your brother and slander your own mother's son" (Psalm 50:20); "They have become filled with every kind of wickedness, evil, greed and depravity. They are full of envy, murder, strife, deceit and malice. They are gossips, slanderers, God-haters, insolent, arrogant and boastful; they invent ways of doing evil" (Romans 1:29-30). James 3:14-16 echoes the charges of Paul from Romans 1 but accuses brothers of being directed by worldly "wisdom," motivated by selfishness and envy. The ensuing disorder and other evil results are also outlined.

What negative comments does James mean? Gossip is negative news about another person: a story of failure or sin being shared with any third party—even if it is true! Slander is just finding fault with another person, not with his actions or ideas but with the character of the person.

In the 1970s, Christians in North America spread a rumor that the corporate symbol of the Proctor and Gamble Company was demonic because it had a moon and some stars in it. The company spent years and a great deal of money trying to defend itself against this false accusation. Well-meaning believers were sharing a slanderous accusation and boycotting a company that was apparently innocent. Unfortunately, the same kind of talk was wrecking the church being addressed here as "brothers" who slandered "one another" (4:11).

James is battling prejudice in the church (2:1-11). These believers treat people differently depending upon their wealth or poverty. Finding fault with people we do not like or are envious of is easy. This is usually done in the form of teasing or joking. But jokes and teasing that include negative images of another person have an edge—they cut.

The command is "Do not slander one another." Why? Speaking evil of your brother makes you his judge. Jesus said, "Do not judge, or you too will be judged" (Matthew 7:1). The command prohibiting negative talk is especially true of Christians. Romans 14:4 asks, "Who are you to judge someone else's servant? To his own master he stands or falls. And he will stand, for the Lord is able to make him stand."

Saul would have been an easy mark for criticism immediately after his conversion. He had been a persecutor, accomplice to murder and an enemy to the Church. But his faith in Christ had brought him God's forgiveness and a new calling. To judge the man who would become Paul, the missionary and apostle to the Gentiles, would have been sitting in judgment on God's servant and breaking His law. Speaking negatively about any Christian makes the person his brother's judge.

Becoming a Judge Makes You a Critic of God's Law (4:11)

"Anyone who speaks against his brother or judges him speaks against the law and judges it. When you judge the law, you are not keeping it, but sitting in judgment on it" (4:11). From the Old Testament to the New Testament, speaking negatively about your brother is forbidden (Leviticus 19:16; Psalm 50:20; 101:5; Proverbs 18:8; 20:19; Romans 1:30; 2 Corinthians 12:20). Negative, critical words and sly insinuations about the character of others is a violation of God's law. The readers of this New Testament letter knew this.

According to his own testimony, my father was not a well-behaved student in high school. In fact, he was a real problem student. Most teachers could find nothing positive to say about him. But one teacher was different. She had a reputation of only saying positive things about people—all people. Another teacher challenged her to say something positive about my father. After some thought and brow-creasing concentration, she said, "He certainly does whistle well."

Christians are commanded to be people of positive words, but we frequently are not. In fact, we are so commonly negative that many of us would question the idea that it is wrong to speak of the faults of a "difficult" person.

What "law" is being broken? The Law of Love (James 2:8)[4]—the specific law James has already mentioned in the context of discrimination against the poor. "Love your neighbor as yourself" is the guiding principle for what you would want others to say about you in the same circumstances. In 4:12, the brother being judged is referred to as a neighbor. Love for your brother and spoken words of judgment are not compatible.

The Golden Rule demands extra grace when believers speak of their enemies. John Wesley was persecuted by mobs, denounced by the clergy of his day and rejected by the church he and his father had served. His reply to this was to love his enemies and to refuse to speak against them.[5] In spite of the excesses and abuses of the church of his day, Wesley spoke only of living a holy life and obeying God. He kept the Law of Love and refused to judge his brothers.

When we judge God's law we insult God. Those who violate these clear commands claim to be greater judges than God. "When you judge the law, you are not keeping it, but sitting in judgment on it" (4:11). Though the believer making the disparaging comments about others might never admit this, his actions say he is putting himself above God's law whenever negative words are spoken about a brother or even an enemy. Judging a brother makes the critic a judge over God's law.

Criticizing God's Law Makes You a Candidate for Judgment (4:12)

God is the only legitimate Judge: "There is only

one Lawgiver and Judge, the one who is able to save and destroy. But you—who are you to judge your neighbor?" (4:12). A constant theme in Scripture, this was also Jesus' doctrine: "Do not judge, or you too will be judged. For in the same way you judge others, you will be judged, and with the measure you use, it will be measured to you" (Matthew 7:1-2).

Judging is God's privilege. You may be asking yourself, *What about the passages that tell us to discern the difference between good and bad fruit in those who may be false prophets?* (e.g., Matthew 7:15-20). *Or what about the passages that command that we not associate with Christians who are immoral and to "judge those inside" the church?* (see 1 Corinthians 5:9-13).

Discerning the difference between good and bad fruit does not mean we must also judge the person. The realm of church discipline is reserved for the spiritual leaders of the church, not for the individual believer. None of these require that anyone speak negatively about his brother in the Lord. The formula for what to say when we find a brother in a sin is clearly outlined by the Lord in Matthew 18 and by Paul in Galatians 6:1-5.

Only God can judge because He alone can save or destroy (Matthew 7:1-5; 10:28; Luke 6:37-42; Romans 2:1; 14:4; 1 Corinthians 4:5; 5:12). Only our omniscient God perfectly understands the actions, events, motivations and thoughts of men (John 2:25; Acts 15:8; Romans 8:27). Only God can be objective, fair, gracious and just in His judgments. Only God can help the sinner or make a saint. Because all this is true, the question James asks should not surprise us.

"But you—who are you to judge your neighbor?"

(James 4:12). This sarcastic question shames us when we judge.[6] The second person "you" makes this a personal rebuke.

We are not Christ who died for sinners to prove His love. In fact, our very lack of love reflects a lack of objectivity and understanding. Unkind words or critical spirits are not from God. The source of such "wisdom" is "earthly, unspiritual, of the devil" (3:15). These words of gossip and criticism come from envy, selfish ambition and personal pride (3:16).

Conclusion

Believers, brothers and sisters, we have an invitation to take a high, holy path that will lead us up out of the rut of speaking negatively about our fellow believers. James has said, "If anyone considers himself religious and yet does not keep a tight reign on his tongue, he deceives himself and his religion is worthless" (1:26). We must not just hear the Word of God today; we must heed it too.

Taming the tongue is the greatest challenge of many believers' lives. But the Holy Spirit can make our words sweet and consistent sources of encouragement, love and righteousness for one another.

If you find fault with your brother, speak first to God to ask if you may be wrong in your opinion. Then go alone to your brother, humbly admitting that you may be mistaken in your understanding of the problem, to ask if your fears may be true (Galatians 6:1-3). Tell no other person about the negative thing you suspect or have observed in your brother until the two of you have tried to correct the problem.

If he does not agree that any wrong has been done

or refuses to repent, Matthew 18:15-18 outlines a process of involving one church leader with you to try to solve the problem, and then more church leaders if these two are unsuccessful. The alternative to this process of reconciliation and careful attention to keeping our tongues under control is a spreading circle of hurt and anger in the body of Christ—as James said, "fights and quarrels among you" (James 4:1).

By speaking only the good we know of one another and keeping in confidence between ourselves and God the negative things we know of each other's past sins, we encourage and build up the church of Christ. Love motivates the speech of a real Christian—all the time and for every other person created in God's image.

Judging others makes us candidates for judgment. "Speak and act as those who are going to be judged by the law that gives freedom, because judgment without mercy will be shown to anyone who has not been merciful. Mercy triumphs over judgment!" (2:12-13). When you speak of one another, be merciful and gracious with your words. Know when just to be quiet and talk to the Lord. God will reward this kind of grace and love with His infinite grace toward you. Refuse to become a judge, a critic of God's law and then a candidate for judgment.

Questions for Reflection or Discussion

1. If you were the professional in the opening illustration and your career, reputation and your relationship with the church was under attack, what would you do? In a booklet titled "Five Vows for Spiritual Power" (Camp Hill, PA: Christian Publications, 1996), A.W. Tozer urges Christians to take

a vow never to defend themselves. "If you turn the defense of yourself over to God He will defend you" (p. 6). Are some of our negative comments about others really a form of self-defense?

2. Are you surprised by the difference between the legal and societal definition of slander and the biblical definition? What is the difference? Whose standard is higher, society's or God's? (See Matthew 5:21-48.)
3. How does James 4:11-17 apply to how we talk about those Christians whose doctrine or behavior is offensive to us?
4. Have you ever thought of yourself as a critic of God's law? Why does speaking negatively of other people make you a judge of the law of God? Why does this practice offend God?
5. On the left side of a piece of paper or an overhead projection, list all the reasons why God is qualified and right to judge men. Now, on the right side, list all the reasons men are not qualified or just to judge one another.

Section B

Surrendered to God's Sovereignty

James 4:13-17

Now listen, you who say, "Today or tomorrow we will go to this or that city, spend a year there, carry on business and make money." Why, you do not even know what will happen tomorrow. What is your life? You are a mist that appears for a little while and then vanishes. Instead, you ought to say, "If it is the Lord's will, we will live and do this or that." As it is, you boast and brag. All such boasting is evil. Anyone, then, who knows the good he ought to do and doesn't do it, sins.

James has just called his readers to submit humbly to God in the area of passing judgment. Christians are not to "play God." In this second section of the lesson, the emphasis changes, but the basic truth remains the same. God is sovereign in His planning for our lives. Our days are ordered by Him. But just as he is tempted to become a judge, man is constantly tempted either to accept credit for what God has done or to make plans independent of God's guidance.

A man planted a beautiful garden. He weeded it, fed it, watered it, defended it from insects and nurtured it until his perfectly straight rows of vegetable plants yielded their abundant harvest. The wife of this super-gardener was a devout Christian. She stood during a church service to praise and thank God for the wonderful garden the Lord had provided for them. At the end of her lengthy words of gratitude to God for their garden, the man stood up. He did not look completely happy. His only words were, "You should have seen the garden when God had it all to Himself."

Who was right and who was wrong? Did God provide the garden or did the sweat and toil of a human's efforts and plans produce the beautiful garden and its abundant crop? If you plan and work hard, can you predict the outcome of your life?

Life Is Uncertain (4:13-14)

> Now listen, you who say, "Today or tomorrow we will go to this or that city, spend a year there, carry on business and make money." Why, you do not even know what will happen tomorrow. What is your life? You are a mist that appears for a little while and then vanishes. (4:13-14)

We make pretentious plans. James confronts businessmen and managers[7] who say things like, "Today or tomorrow we will make money." Although these businessmen are the focus of this segment of the letter, any person making future plans would be included in the exhortation of these verses.

If this is true, the judgment of the author applies to anyone making pronouncements about his intended goals for the future. If a newly married couple said, "We plan to have three children, pay for our home in ten years and retire at sixty-five," they would be just as affected by these words as any businessman. A student who plans to graduate in four years and pursue a particular career, an athlete who predicts a certain level of success in his sport, or even a church that plans to grow or build or reach a certain number of people can be saying similar things: "Today or tomorrow, we will go to this or that city . . . and . . ." (4:13).

Why is this a problem? The problem is still the use of the tongue and the attitude of the heart these words reveal. Whom does the speaker trust to make his plans succeed? When we presume that our plans will be fruitful and don't acknowledge God, our focus is upon human effort and its fruits. Notice the emphasis: "*We* will go. . . . *We* make money. . . . *We* will carry on business."

My wife and I moved to a new part of the country to begin a new church. We and our denominational leaders had a great plan for building a solid core of more than 100 people in less than three years. The church would be self-supporting by then and ready to really grow. Perhaps we had the idea that God must make believers' plans succeed.

But God has only promised to bless and grant success to *His* plans, not ours. We do not automatically know God's plans for us in advance. The church closed and we were forced to move to another ministry. During the next ten years, God did raise that church up under new leadership and with a different plan. Often when wisdom is required, "you do not have, because you do not ask God. When you ask, you do not receive, because you ask with wrong motives, that you may spend what you get on your pleasures" (4:2-3).

We do not know the future; life is uncertain. Verse 14 parallels the truth of Proverbs 27:1: "Do not boast about tomorrow, for you do not know what a day may bring forth." Only God knows the future, even one day in advance.

Leaving this key element out of planning is pretending that we know what the tomorrows of our lives will produce. This is an attitude of independence from God. A personal question follows for the would-be planner: "What is your life?" (James 4:14).

How should Christians approach the future and planning? Should they give up planning altogether? How can we take the realities of life's uncertainty into account? We could pretend that the garden is ours alone and that we can grow what we want when we want. But that is a foolish attitude. What we ought to do is pray and trust God, believing that success or failure belongs to our Lord. The husband who took the credit and the wife who praised God for their garden represent the two points of view James contrasts in this section.

Your life is uncertain. It is "a mist, a vapor."[8] The words "appears" and "vanishes" indicate the shortness and unpredictability of life.[9] Planning without reference to God is foolish,[10] because we have no guarantee of even one more day on the planet.

Life Is under God's Control (4:15)

This verse answers the question of how the believer's attitude in planning should sound: "Instead, you ought to say, 'If it is the Lord's will, we will live and do this or that' " (4:15). Jesus' parable of the rich fool, found in Luke 12:16-21, is teaching the same truth:

> The ground of a certain rich man produced a good crop. He thought to himself, "What shall I do? I have no place to store my crops."
>
> Then he said, "This is what I'll do. I will tear down my barns and build bigger ones. . . ."
>
> But God said to him, "You fool! This very night your life will be demanded from you. Then who will get what you have prepared for yourself?"
>
> This is how it will be with anyone who stores up things for himself but is not rich toward God.

Greed and arrogant self-reliance are never blessed by God. God demanded the rich fool's life; His judgment falls upon selfishness and self-reliance. The man was living as if God did not exist. Making plans without reference to God's will amounts to "practical atheism."[11] Like the man who thought his garden was all his own doing, the rich fool thought his success and all its fruits belonged to him alone.

Job was a wise man. He gave God credit for his success and had faith even through his suffering and loss. He said, "The LORD gave and the LORD has taken away" (Job 1:21). When God made Job wealthy, he gave the Lord the glory for his success. And when he lost his property, his family and his reputation, Job still trusted that God's plan was being fulfilled.

James is not condemning making plans. "If it is the Lord's will, we will live and do this or that" (James 4:15). A future element of planning exists in the suggested "you ought to say." But the difference now is that the plan is under the control of God's perfect will. Phrases like "and God permitting" or "if it is the Lord's will" are found in several places in Scripture (Hebrews 6:3; 1 Corinthians 4:19). The same attitude toward the future is found in Jesus' prayer in the Garden of Gethsemane, "May your will be done" (Matthew 26:42).

Planning is good and helpful if it includes praying for God's direction and His purposes to be fulfilled. "Unless the LORD builds the house, its builders labor in vain. Unless the LORD watches over the city, the watchmen stand guard in vain" (Psalm 127:1). We will do what God allows, no more. Christians' attitudes in planning and in speaking of plans must include this key truth.

"If the Lord wills" is not intended to become a mantra Christians recite without meaning.[12] Often people have picked this up as a kind of good luck charm in words. Or it is used to get out of doing things we have no intention to do. When you invite someone to attend church and he says, "If God wills," he usually really means, "Unless God wakes me, dresses me and drives me to church Himself, I will not be there." We are unwilling to do much of what God wills that we do.

When any believer speaks of future plans, he must acknowledge God's control of that future. He must be willing to do what God reveals as His perfect will. The righteous language of a follower of Christ includes the possibility that our will and the Lord's will for us may not be the same thing. "If it is the Lord's will, we will live and do this or that" (James 4:15). Life is under God's control.

Life Is Surrendered to God's Sovereignty (4:16-17)

"As it is, you boast and brag. All such boasting is evil. Anyone, then, who knows the good he ought to do and doesn't do it, sins" (4:16-17). The second person pronoun "you" emphasizes that this is not merely a hypothetical problem.

Christians frequently sound pious about their lives and God's relationship to them and about what they or their church has accomplished. When any believer talks as if he is in charge,[13] he boasts and brags. ("You should have seen the garden when God had it to Himself.") "As it is" indicates that this was the current attitude of the readers as the letter was being written.

Man always wants some credit for success. In our hearts we tend to take credit for everything from how good-looking our children are to our athletic ability. I was thankful when, during a 1996 interview, the Olympic champion of the decathlon, Dan O'Brien, gave God and all the people who supported and coached him the credit for his gold medal.

Bragging or taking credit in our hearts is "evil." James pronounces God's judgment against such talk. Leaving God out of our celebrations is wrong. Perhaps the gardener's wife in the story should have acknowledged her husband's hard work more. But she was absolutely correct to give God the glory for a great garden. She knew that "every good and perfect gift is from above, coming down from the Father" (1:17). This is true!

To avoid evil and pursue holiness, a Christian's words must reflect this truth. A.W. Tozer said, "*Never accept any glory*. God is jealous of His glory and He will not give His glory to another. He will not even share His glory with another."[14]

The proverb of James 4:17 is universal in its application. "Anyone, then, who knows the good he ought to do and doesn't do it, sins." The commentaries have debated about why this proverb is placed at just this point in the argument, with some even postulating that this is not connected in any way to the context.[15]

But James often uses proverbial sayings to bring his points home.[16] The "good [we] ought to do" (4:17) is to put our lives under God's control, to surrender in our hearts to His sovereignty. Followers of Christ must form their future plans under an umbrella of prayer, seeking God's will more than their own. The future must be submitted to God's providence and sovereign control. Any "boasting" we do must be about our gracious God and His acts of love.

God desires to be consulted and acknowledged in planning, and not including Him is "sin"—the final word of the chapter. The slightly shocking ending emphasizes how serious God is about our attitude toward future plans. To acknowledge God's sovereign control over all the tomorrows of our lives is good and right. Submitting our lives to the protecting, guiding hand of the Father is righteous. Leaving these things out of our planning is sin! James has carefully outlined the good thing we ought to do; all that remains for us is to live up to God's standard and acknowledge Him as the Lord of all our future plans.

Conclusion

Life is uncertain. Our world is full of palm readers,

stargazers and psychics who are seeking to predict the future. But the deeper life of a believer is a life of dependence upon the love of God for the future. Psalm 31:15 wisely acknowledges, "My times are in your hands." Faith lives in peace about God's plan for what will happen tomorrow.

Life is under God's control. While some movements seek to teach that "if it is Your will" reflects a lack of faith, the opposite is actually true. Seeking the will of God in our lives is faith in *God* rather than faith in what we seek from Him.

The deeper life is a life of complete surrender. It is a life submitted wholly to God for His purposes. That is the "good life" Christ desires for His people. The glory for such a life belongs to God alone.

Questions for Reflection or Discussion

1. Why is making plans without praying for God's will so common among Christians?
2. Look into Gideon's battle plan (Judges 7), Israel's plan to conquer Jericho (Joshua 6) or the plan of Christ to die on the cross. What would you have said about these plans of God if you had been part of Gideon's army, Joshua's exiles or Jesus' disciples? What can you learn from these examples about God's way of planning?
3. Christians and their churches often make predictions about goals they will reach by a certain date. Is this right or wrong? How does the part of James 4:14 which says, "Why, you do not even know what will happen tomorrow" apply to this kind of prediction? What should we say about the future plans we make?

4. Have you ever said, "if it's the Lord's will" without meaning it? If so, under what circumstances?
5. Why is it evil to say what we will do and when we will do it without any reference to the will of God? Does the word "evil" sound too strong to you in this circumstance?
6. What other "good things" are there in James that we ought to do which 4:17 applies to? Are sins of omission easier or more difficult to avoid than sins of commission? Why?

Endnotes

1. Arndt and Gingrich, *A Greek-English Lexicon*, 413.
2. Ropes, *Saint James,* 274
3. Arndt and Gingrich, *A Greek-English Lexicon*, 413.
4. Ibid., 163.
5. Garth Lean, *Strangely Warmed* (Wheaton, IL: Tyndale, 1964), 77-96.
6. Adamson, *Epistle of James,* 178.
7. Martin, *James,* 160, 165.
8. Davids, *Epistle of James,* 122.
9. Arndt and Gingrich, *A Greek-English Lexicon,* 14.
10. Moo, *James,* 167.
11. Adamson, *Epistle of James,* 180.
12. Martin, *James,* 167.
13. Davids, *Epistle of James,* 123.
14. A.W. Tozer, "Five Vows for Spiritual Power" (Camp Hill, PA: Christian Publications, 1996), 9.
15. Dibelius, *James,* 230, 235.
16. Martin, *James,* 168.

Lesson 9

James 5:1-6

Provided with the Opportunity to Give

James 5:1-6

Now listen, you rich people, weep and wail because of the misery that is coming upon you. Your wealth has rotted, and moths have eaten your clothes. Your gold and silver are corroded. Their corrosion will testify against you and eat your flesh like fire. You have hoarded wealth in the last days. Look! The wages you failed to pay the workmen who mowed your fields are crying out against you. The cries of the harvesters have reached the ears of the Lord Almighty. You have lived on earth in luxury and self-indulgence. You have fattened yourselves in the day of slaughter. You have condemned and murdered innocent men, who were not opposing you.

North Americans feed enough fish to their cats each year to supply protein for a starving Third World country.[1] We spend eighteen times more money to feed pets and sixty times more on alcohol than we spend to reach the world for Christ. The money we spend on cosmetics annually is more than we give as a nation to reach the lost world for Christ.[2] The average church-attending family will spend more money eating out in restaurants this year than they will give to the work of Christ.[3]

The passage we are studying is directed to wealthy farmers who are probably not part of the church to whom James is writing.[4] Then why write these words to the church? The passage is intended to comfort suffering Christians who are the victims of the economic policies of a wealthy, self-indulgent culture. This passage, like Psalm 58, first condemns the unrighteous and then comforts the righteous in the next section (James 5:7-11).[5]

The church in North America is part of such a culture. The churches of major cities and their suburbs around the world are often filled with a relatively more wealthy group of believers than their rural neighbors. It affects the way we live and the way we give. Let's see if God may be speaking to us along with the other wealthy people described here.

Hoarding Wealth Is Not God's Plan (5:1-3)

> Now listen, you rich people, weep and wail because of the misery that is coming upon you. Your wealth has rotted, and moths have eaten your clothes. Your gold and silver are corroded. Their corrosion will testify against you and eat your flesh like fire. You have hoarded wealth in the last days. (5:1-3)

"Now listen, you rich people" applies to all North Americans. We don't think we're very rich. After all, there is always someone more wealthy than we are to compare our income to. The wealthy people to whom this is addressed also would probably not have admitted that the passage referred to them.

Even people living at the poverty level in North America are "rich people" by Third World standards. In 1995, the average annual income of a Christian in Mali, West Africa was somewhere around $300 U.S. In a place like Indonesia, the average income may be twice that amount. Most of the population of the world lives far below the poverty line with little or no access to medical care, adequate food or an education. Though we prefer to only compare our income to those who have more and cry poverty, we are rich people!

Although the poor, persecuted Jewish believers were the focus of the letter, not every first-century believer was impoverished. James does not condemn the wealthy as such, but he does condemn the misuse of wealth. Those who refuse to acknowledge God with their possessions, who are selfish with their wealth, are instructed here concerning their future plight. Judgment is pronounced upon those who hoard riches. "Weep and wail because of the misery that is coming upon you" (5:1). Doom is certain and constitutes a legitimate reason for grief and fear in the present.

Condemnation of the decadent rich is a prophetic theme of both the Old and New Testaments. The teaching of Jesus includes pronouncements of woe on those who selfishly spend all that God gives them on themselves. Luke 6:24-26 says,

But woe to you who are rich,
for you have already received your comfort.
Woe to you who are well fed now,
for you will go hungry.
Woe to you who laugh now,
for you will mourn and weep.
Woe to you when all men speak well of you,
for that is how their fathers treated the false prophets.

Misery is coming, and no attempt is made here to avert it. No counsel is given for the right use of wealth in this passage. James is usually quick to give a corrective word, but in this case, there is only condemnation and a certain announcement of coming judgment.

Hoarded goods will testify against the rich: "Your wealth has rotted, and moths have eaten your clothes. Your gold and silver are corroded. Their corrosion will testify against you and eat your flesh like fire. You have hoarded wealth in the last days" (James 5:2-3).

First-century wealth usually consisted of "grain, gold and garments."[6] The word translated "wealth" could also be translated "food."[7] The wealth of people in this time was in these material things but also a richness of power (see 5:5-6).

The first of the charges leveled at the rich people being addressed is that they have hoarded wealth that is worthless.

The present perfect tense usually indicates a present reality which is the result of a past action: "rotted . . . moths have eaten . . . corroded." But it is not literally true that the wealth of the wealthy is rotted, moth-eaten and rusty. One commentator considers the tense a form of "prophetic anticipation"[8]—not having actually occurred yet. This is what will happen to the wealth of the readers when they face God's judgment, emphasizing the temporal nature of all earthly riches.

Jesus counsels,

> Sell your possessions and give to the poor. Provide purses for yourselves that will not wear out, a treasure in heaven that will not be exhausted, where no thief comes near and no moth destroys. For where your treasure is, there your heart will be also. (Luke 12:33-34)

Earthly wealth is temporary. It wears out, breaks, gets stolen and used up.

Another possible reason the perfect tense is used here is that the readers might have had more things than they could either use or care for. Their food rotted before they could eat it all. Moths were eating all the clothing they hoarded but could not wear.[9]

Sound familiar? We throw away food from refrigerators because it has been there so long that it is no longer edible (or even recognizable). The dumpsters behind restaurants and grocery stores in North America are filled daily with unsold food. Clothing goes out of style before it is worn enough to wear out. Hoarding is simply accumulating more than a household can use.

Technically speaking, gold does not rust or corrode. Silver tarnishes but does not generally oxidize enough to lose its value. James is observing that gold and silver have no value in eternity, except perhaps symbolically as street-paving material (Revelation 21:21).

Ironically, the "treasure" these rich people have accumulated is actually multiplied judgment. The only thing that hoarding material wealth earns in eternity is abundant judgment.[10] "You have hoarded wealth in the last days" (James 5:3). The "last days" are here! Judgment is imminent for those who are selfish.[11] In light of this fact, to hoard things which cannot be taken into eternity as treasures when this life ends is foolishness.

Every fall the western United States experiences wildfires. The nation watches annually as brave firemen seek to bring the blazes under control before they destroy homes and lives. Knowing that judgment comes to the selfish and yet continuing to ignore the danger is like stockpiling gasoline at your cabin during the fire season. Hoarding wealth instead of sharing it or using it for the kingdom of God fuels the fire of judgment hotter for the one who hoards when he should help those with less. "Their corrosion will testify against you and eat your flesh like fire" (5:3).

God Hears the Cries of the Poor (5:4)

"Look! The wages you failed to pay the workmen who mowed your fields are crying out against you. The cries of the harvesters have reached the ears of the Lord Almighty" (5:4).

All the workers in Third World sweatshops making our clothes, the people making our cars who earn next to nothing and the migrant workers and immigrants who harvest our crops in this country cry out to God. Some of them are Christians. Many of the believers who protested for democracy in China are now in labor camps making the things the Western world buys.[12]

God has heard the cries of the oppressed workers, says James. Poor believers in his time sometimes had to sell themselves into slavery to survive. The book of Philemon is an appeal for grace on behalf of a Christian slave named Onesimus. The oppressed can be comforted that their injustices have been seen; God cares when no one else does. The next section of chapter 5 (verses 7-11) is God's comfort to suffering believers until Christ's return.

The wealthy do not like to look at such ugly truth. But the passage says, "Look!" (5:4). James often uses this word to emphasize important points.[13] The wealthy must be careful not to look the other way.

A popular television personality and professed believer was shocked and saddened when she learned from a congressional lobbyist that a major retail chain was having her line of children's clothing manufactured by child labor under terrible conditions.

The rich are often insulated from the working conditions of their employees! Remember the shock and anger of Moses when he first discovered the mistreatment of his people in Egypt (Exodus 2:11-12). But this charge against the rich is worse than ignorance. The poor are not only lacking what they need; they are not even being given what they are owed: "wages you failed to pay" (James 5:4). The fair proceeds of their work, their promised earnings are being withheld.

For a modern example of this, think about companies that have a policy of laying off workers just before they are eligible to receive their retirement benefits. Loyal employees worked for years, trusting that they could retire with their pensions, only to be cheated out of them at the last moment.

On the other hand, the factory of a man named Aaron Fuerstein from Mulden, Massachusetts burned down on December 11, 1995. He made the national news when he paid his workers for thirty days even though he had lost his business and they could not work to earn that money.

Testimony will rise up to God based upon how the rich believer treats those who labor for him. He will face the Judge of the whole earth who has heard the cries of cheated employees. Or perhaps this wealthy believer will hear how God was praised because of his generosity and fairness. Prophets have always condemned those who did not treat employees fairly: "Woe to him who builds his palace by unrighteousness, his upper rooms by injustice, making his countrymen work for nothing, not paying them for their labor" (Jeremiah 22:13).

Helping the Needy Is Preventing God's Reproof (5:5-6)

"You have lived on earth in luxury and self-indulgence. You have fattened yourselves in the day of slaughter. You have condemned and murdered innocent men, who were not opposing you" (James 5:5-6). The descriptive words delineating a life of "luxury and self-indulgence" condemn the wealthy in this passage. Ownership is not their problem; an uncaring life is.

William Shakespeare described those who keep acquiring long after their needs are met as a "tub both full and running" (Cymbeline, I.6). "How much is enough?" would have been a worthy question for those accused here. The deeper life is defined as much by what a person keeps as by what he gives.

When do we have enough to share, to help others with less?

Speaking earlier of the desire of the rich to spend all that was received on themselves, James cited one reason for unanswered prayer: selfishly spending all we get on our own pleasures (4:3).

"Greed" is the best one-word description of the life God condemns here. Such a life leads to God's eternal reproof: death. Passing by the brother or sister in deep need with only a Christian platitude is not faith or love (2:14-17; Luke 10:33ff). "Faith without deeds is useless" (James 2:20).

The sentence that follows elicits a familiar and graphic image: "You have fattened yourselves in the day of slaughter" (5:5). My grandfather raised cattle to sell for the beef market. When he wanted to get the best price from the sale of an animal that would become steak, he fed that beef more than any other animal until it was the fattest one he owned. The animal was put in a small yard and did not need to walk far to find the best food, water and shelter. It was protected from work and stress. Why? So it would be more tender when it was eaten. This picture of a self-indulgent life that cares for no one else but only for its own comfort is likened to the lifestyle of that special beef "fattened [for] the day of slaughter."

James returns to the second person, "you." His fourth accusation is the most serious of them all. "You have condemned and murdered innocent men, who were not opposing you" (5:6). How? The wealthy and powerful of the day, like the Sadducees, took advantage of the poor with impunity using the legal system of Rome and Jerusalem.[14] One perversion of the

Golden Rule says, "Those with the gold make the rules." Those with the most money also have the most power. Present examples from the corporate world allow the powerful to hire the best attorneys when they are doing a hostile takeover of another company. They can defraud the poor of their land and their labor without facing any earthly justice.

Some think the next phrase "innocent men" refers to Christ, the righteous One. Others believe James is the innocent one prophetically predicting his own martyrdom.[15] The most likely interpretation says it could be unnamed poor men, women and children who suffer and die all over the world due to the injustices and inequities imposed upon them by the wealthy.

The root word for "murdered" is not a figurative word; it is literally "to take a life, condemn, kill."[16] Persecuted believers in Christ often lost their income, property, freedom and even their lives. The stoning of Stephen (Acts 7) and the deep persecution that followed by men like Saul who "was still breathing out murderous threats against the Lord's disciples" (9:1) indicate that the persecution of the Church was both physical and economic.

The "innocent" who suffer from the economic practices of the wealthy of their culture are not limited to those suffering persecution for their faith. James has already mentioned widows and orphans as the recipients of the grace of true Christians (James 1:27). The most needy people of any age do not oppose the wealthy because they have no means to defend themselves or to effectively oppose anyone.[17]

Conclusion

James has leveled four accusations against the wealthy of his day and of ours:

1. They hoard wealth instead of helping the poor or doing the work of God with it.

2. They are dishonest in refusing to pay their employees a fair wage for their work.

3. They have fallen into the trap of self-indulgence when God has blessed them in order that they could bless others.

4. Their policies and practices end up leading to the death of innocent people.

God's judgment is certain and imminent upon lives filled with greed and selfishness. God will resist the proud and give grace to the humble. His plan is that Christians help, not hoard. The plan of God is to redeem and rescue the righteous, rather than reproving them in the Day of Judgment. Which life will you choose today? How can you and I share more of what God has blessed us with? How can we express the "pure and faultless" religion (1:27) that shares the things God has entrusted to us with the helpless and the poor?

Questions for Reflection or Discussion

1. Do you believe that this passage applies to the Christians of the Western world in this century? Why or why not?
2. Many of us are guilty of collecting more food and clothing than we can use. Is this wastefulness ac-

ceptable to our society? Is it acceptable to God? How could we prevent wasting food? clothing? What should we do with the money we save?

3. What might 5:3 refer to when it states that "your gold and silver are corroded"? How does the parable of the talents (Matthew 25:14-30) help answer this question? Why does God give some people more than they need?
4. How much responsibility do Christians have to find out if the items they purchase were produced through Third World sweatshops or child labor? How can we know if our money is supporting some evil practices?
5. Might the principle in James 5:4 apply in any way to your church?
6. As some recent books and articles in Christian periodicals have accused, does the North American evangelical Church live "in luxury and self-indulgence"? What is the difference between being "a rich man" and living "in luxury and self-indulgence"?
7. The accusation "You have condemned and murdered innocent men, who were not opposing you" (5:6) could certainly be applied to the policies of many world governments. How can it be applied to our culture?
8. Is there a way for individuals to avoid the judgment promised in this passage? What about the nation where you live?

Endnotes

1. For these statistics, see Nov/Dec '95 *The Loose Change Newsletter.*
2. Rev. Marvin Parker in a message at the 1997 World Missions Workshop, Black Forest Conference Center, Colorado Springs, CO.
3. Ron Sider, *Rich Christians in an Age of Hunger* (Downers Grove, IL: InterVarsity Press, 1977), 39-56.
4. Martin, *James*, 172-173.
5. Adamson, *Epistle of James,* 184.
6. Mayor, *Epistle of James,* 149.
7. Adamson, *Epistle of James,* 184.
8. Ibid.,185.
9. Moo, *James*, 161-162.
10. Ibid.,162.
11. Martin, *James,* 178.
12. See Paul Marshall's book, *Their Blood Cries Out* (Dallas: Word Books, 1997) for an excellent resource on suffering Christians around the world.
13. Davids, *Epistle of James,* 177.
14. Martin, *James,* 180.
15. Ibid., 182, 184.
16. Kittel, *TDNT,* vol. 3, 621-622.
17. Adamson, *Epistle of James,* 188.

Lesson 10

James 5:7-12

Section A

Encouraged to Be Patient Until Christ's Return

James 5:7-11

Be patient, then, brothers, until the Lord's coming. See how the farmer waits for the land to yield its valuable crop and how patient he is for the autumn and spring rains. You too, be patient and stand firm, because the Lord's coming is near. Don't grumble against each other, brothers, or you will be judged. The Judge is standing at the door!

Brothers, as an example of patience in the face of suffering, take the prophets who spoke in the name of the Lord. As you know, we consider blessed those who have persevered. You have heard of Job's perseverance and have seen what the Lord finally brought about. The Lord is full of compassion and mercy.

How do you deal with the stress of life? Do you tend to lose patience with it all? How often do you say, "There is a limit to my patience!" Do you tend to grow irritable and begin to blame others when life is difficult? Have you tried some shortcuts to help God along and to extricate yourself from your trying circumstances?

If any of these sound familiar to you, you are in step with the church to whom James wrote these words. The following is a call to patience and faithful endurance in the face of suffering. Christians at the time of this writing were usually both poor and persecuted. Help would not come from the government, either the local Jewish one or the distant Roman government. They must wait for the hand of God to move to bring back their true king, Jesus Christ.

The return of Christ will bring both judgment for the godless who were persecuting them (5:1-6) and deliverance for the righteous believer.[1] Two attributes of the deeper Christian life are courageous, persistent faith and confident expectation of the return of Christ. These two virtues are the answer to victorious living in a difficult and hostile world.

Be Patient Until the Lord's Coming (5:7-8)

Here the call to patience is issued to believers (5:7). James mentions "brothers" three times in five verses. This call to patience is only for Christians. Patience is the fruit of the Holy Spirit (Galatians 5:22) in the life of a surrendered Christian. Only those living in accord with the Spirit of God will actually evidence this character trait of the kingdom.

Three times the text commands, "Be patient." Two different words are used in the original language of the passage: the first word is used in James 5:7, 8 and 10; the second is used only in verse 11, translated "persevere." They can be synonyms, but here the first word implies "patient waiting" and the second, "fortitude," the strength that comes from patience.[2]

What is patience? Patience is not "stoic fatalism" or "pious resignation."[3] Biblical patience, Holy Spirit patience, is the ability to wait on God in the midst of suffering and not deny your faith. Patience is the ability to glorify God even while you are suffering. Fanny Crosby wrote some of the greatest hymns of our faith during the years of her agonizing illness. That was patience lived out in the midst of pain.

"Until the Lord's coming"—the Parousia is brought to the attention of the readers two times. The expectation of Christ's imminent return continues through the latter half of the fifth chapter. For James, "the last days" had already arrived (James 5:3).

The Lord's return, the Parousia, is a constant reminder to actually live a holy life. Many texts link sanctification and the return of Christ (e.g., 1 Thessalonians 5:23-24). Albert Simpson, founder of The Christian and Missionary Alliance, taught that sanctification is preparation for the return of Christ, and that the Second Coming is the complement of sanctification.[4] Christ's work in the life of the believer will be completed when the Lord returns.

"Until the Lord's coming" (James 5:7) is the answer to both why and how long believers are to practice patience.[5] For persecuted Christians suffering under the thumb of Roman occupation and Jewish persecution, the time of suffering had a limit. Patience was encouraged by both the limited duration of suffering and by the fact that their Lord would return one day to redeem the righteous.

The farmer planting a crop illustrates the need for and an example of biblical patience (5:7). Planting and cultivation of crops was an everyday occurrence in Palestine and essential to life. Planting implies faith in a harvest and requires patience until the crop matures. No amount of begging or pleading or the threat of force could make a garden grow any faster. Farmers could go hungry as they waited for the food in their garden to grow and ripen enough to eat. They worked hard and waited every day in hope for the time when their faithfulness plus God's rain would produce "its valuable crop." Life-sustaining food or starvation hung in the balance while the farmer and the community waited.

Rash human effort will not hasten Christ's return nor will it bring an end to the world's injustices. Some commentaries state that these words imply that the church was tempted to use force to get what it wanted (1:20, 3:15-16; 4:1-10).[6] They could have followed the course of the zealots in the Jewish community seeking to make change through physical violence, using selfish ambition, disorder, fighting, quarreling and even killing to advance Christ's cause. The Crusades and the Spanish Inquisition are dark blots on the history of the Church resulting from such misguided zeal.

Impatience leads to anger and a lack of trust in God. Learning to wait patiently until the seasons bring the rain of God's blessing is difficult in every generation of believers, but even more so for those suffering persecution. No amount of picketing, protesting, petitioning or political activism would relieve the pain of these believers. Becoming zealots or insurrectionists would not help them. They were to wait upon God for their deliverance.

"You too, be patient and stand firm, because the Lord's coming is near" (5:8). Our lives must be lived in light of Christ's return.

> For the grace of God that brings salvation has appeared to all men. It teaches us to say "No" to ungodliness and worldly passions, and to live self-controlled, upright and godly lives in this present age, while we wait for the blessed hope—the glorious appearing of our great God and Savior, Jesus Christ. (Titus 2:11-13)

"Stand firm" is a call to a life of sanctification and persevering faith while believers patiently wait for Christ's return.

The Parousia is "near." James sees Christ's return as soon, close, coming at any moment. This is not the time for believers to take their plight into their own hands by some rash action. The call is for an understanding that "the Lord's coming is near." Be patient until the Lord comes.

Be Patient Until the Lord Judges (5:9)

"Don't grumble against each other, brothers, or you will be judged. The Judge is standing at the door!" (5:9). To grumble is literally to "groan," but here the word is used to mean "complaining, blaming others."[7] To "grumble against each other" is the most common reaction to pain. Nurses experience the complaints and anger of their patients daily even when the patient's pain has nothing to do with his nurse's care. When saints suffer, they are tempted to blame other believers for their troubles.

The blame game is forbidden here. James 4:11-12 commands the readers to stop slandering and judging one another. Hearing Christians criticizing and blaming one another for their discomforts and disappointments was already too common.

The promise is here, "Don't grumble against each other . . . or you will be judged" (5:9). You will receive the same treatment you give, and you will be guilty of playing God. Condemning others or complaining about other Christians leads to condemnation from God! Jesus said, "Do not judge, or you too will be judged" (Matthew 7:1). Christians are not the source of life's troubles. "Brothers" are the family of all true followers of Christ and not their enemies.

"The Judge is standing at the door!" (James 5:9). The emphasis of this metaphor is "not the length of time between the present and the return of Christ, but how Christians must deal with the interim of time until He comes."[8]

When my brother and I were children, we shared a bedroom. After our father had told us to be quiet for the night, we would sometime disobey, laughing and talking. Then we would hear his footsteps as he came down the hall to our bedroom door. Although he did not speak or enter the room, the idea that our father was just outside the door, only a second away, changed our behavior. The threat of imminent discipline encouraged us suddenly to become obedient children.

Jesus Christ is just outside the door of history. The

Holy Son of God is going to judge every believer according to what he has done. "You, then, why do you judge your brother? Or why do you look down on your brother? For we will all stand before God's judgment seat" (Romans 14:10). The command to "brothers" to stop blaming one another as they expectantly look for the Lord's return is ample incentive for repentance. Patiently waiting for God to judge between the believer and his brothers is imperative. Christ will judge; that is His exclusive right.

Be Patient Until the Lord Comforts (5:10-11)

> Brothers, as an example of patience in the face of suffering, take the prophets who spoke in the name of the Lord. As you know, we consider blessed those who have persevered. You have heard of Job's perseverance and have seen what the Lord finally brought about. The Lord is full of compassion and mercy. (James 5:10-11)

James now gives some biblical examples of the fruit of the Spirit he has commanded listeners to produce by faith. These are examples of "patience in the face of suffering," a technical phrase, the purpose of which is to underscore the importance of patience and to show the Christian community that patience is a common characteristic of God's greatest servants.[9]

"As an example . . . take the prophets"—readers were familiar with the stories of the Old Testament prophets from Scripture since they were read each week in the synagogues. Various prophets would have come to mind as appropriate examples of patience in the face of tribulation. I think of Jeremiah, the weeping prophet, who was faithful to God in spite of being hated by the people he loved, being branded a traitor, ignored in his efforts to save his nation, starved, humiliated, imprisoned by his own leaders and finally taken into captivity by a foreign power. During all this, he faithfully spoke for God and praised Him—"patience in the face of suffering."

Hebrews 11 gives more examples of such faithfulness. Jesus Christ is the ultimate example of "patience in the face of suffering." Even Christ, "for the joy set before him endured the cross, scorning its shame, and sat down at the right hand of the throne of God" (Hebrews 12:2).

Job is the second example James gives reference to. The "patience of Job" has become proverbial over the centuries. But Job was not an example of suffering in silence; some people object to him as an example of patience! After all, Job complained bitterly to God (Job 7:11-16; 10:18). But Job never ceased to believe in God. As William Barclay has said, "Though Job complained, the flame of faith was never extinguished in his heart."[10]

The most important part of the race is the finish line; to win, you must finish. In the 1996 Olympics in Atlanta, Georgia, a new world record was set in the 200-meter race. Michael Johnson stumbled on the seventh step of the race. He won the gold medal because he patiently kept running, finishing the race and improving his performance with every step after his mistake.

Job finished well too. Speaking of persecution, Jesus said, "All men will hate you because of me, but he who stands firm to the end will be saved" (Matthew 10:22). Job concluded his time of suffering praising God's faithfulness and perfect wisdom and repenting of his words of complaint (Job 42:1-6).

"And [you] have seen what the Lord finally brought about" (James 5:11). Referred to as "the end" in the original language, the New International Version translation is correct in rendering this as an objective genitive, meaning that the final blessing of Job was the object of God's actions, "the end" result of God's plan.[11] The final blessing of God on Job's life took two forms: physically God gave him twice what he had lost in his trials (Job 42:10), but more importantly, Job received God's blessing as the Father called Job "My servant." Eternal life and God's glory through Job's life were the larger plan of God. This "harvest of righteousness" (Hebrews 12:11) was the plan of God for Job's life. This "end" reminds suffering believers that God is in charge, even when His servants suffer.

"The Lord is full of compassion and mercy" (James 5:11). How can James confidently make this statement of God's kindness to Christians who are in pain? The view of the letter is that God is more concerned with His children's eternal welfare than with their present comfort. God wants His children holy more than He wants them happy. Trouble, then persevering faith and then maturity and wholeness in Christ is the progression of the deeper Christian life (1:2-4, 12). God's reason for allowing suffering is to produce mature, Christlike people, to refine the saints like gold.

"As you know, we consider blessed those who have persevered" (5:11). The verb tense here indicates that

James is referring only to those who have stood fast until the end of their lives.[12] "The crown of life" is waiting for the believer who "perseveres under trial" (1:12).

This addresses the problem question, "Why do righteous people experience suffering?" God loves us enough to remove the impurities from our lives, to make us holy. So trials are God's grace in action purifying His children. "God disciplines us for our good, that we may share in his holiness" (Hebrew 12:10). Christ's mercy forgives when trials produce repentance; His Spirit cleanses and sanctifies those who persevere by faith.

Conclusion

Jesus Christ is coming again. Be patient until the Lord returns. Wait like a farmer, in faith and hope, for the harvest of righteousness Christ will bring. Wait for the Judge of all the earth to come to establish His justice for the ungodly who have oppressed God's people. Be patient with one another. Refuse to judge, criticize or blame other believers.

Be patient and persevering in your stand for Christ until the Lord's comfort finds you faithful and holy at our Lord's return. God has a plan. Patience and steadfastness require courage and spiritual toughness. Ask Christ to deepen and purify your life as you stand firm in Christ through faith.

Questions for Reflection or Discussion

1. How does the call to be patient until the Lord's coming affect your attitude toward life's difficulties? What is patience from a biblical viewpoint?

How is it different from the kind of patience that men exhibit in their own strength? Can you think of some examples of this fruit of the Holy Spirit in the lives of other Christians?

2. The farmer illustration points to the need to wait for God's hand to produce a crop; how does all the technology of irrigation, modern pest control and scientific methods impact the effectiveness of this illustration?
3. In what situations do Christians blame other Christians for their difficulties? Why is this wrong?
4. How does the imminence of Christ's return affect the way you live the Christian life? How should it affect your walk with God that "the Judge is standing at the door"?
5. Why do we need examples of men and women who have been "patient in the face of suffering"? What did Jesus promise His followers about suffering? Can you think of any other passages that promise that the faithful believer will endure persecution or suffering?
6. Those who persevere "we consider blessed." Why not consider blessed all those who suffer? How did the suffering of men like Jeremiah and Job affect the world for God's purposes? How did their relationship with God change during the time of their discomfort? How have you grown during times of trouble and testing?
7. What is God's purpose in allowing His people to suffer? How can God be "full of compassion and mercy" when His people are being persecuted?

Section B

Characterized by Integrity

James 5:12

Above all, my brothers, do not swear—not by heaven or by earth or by anything else. Let your "Yes" be yes, and your "No," no, or you will be condemned.

Accompanying the thought that we must patiently await the return of Christ and the day of judgment and redemption is the idea that God is the only One who can make promises and know that He can keep them. Christ has promised to return. God has stated, upon the credibility of an unchanging character, that He will save those who come to Him in faith. God's Word is certain. The second part of this lesson continues the promise of judgment for another form of verbal sin. Just as impatient grumbling leads to judgment, so do reckless promises.

Chapter 8 of William Bennett's book *The Book of Virtues* is dedicated to honesty. In the introduction to the chapter, Bennett refers to the parental habit of saying to our children, "Don't let me catch you doing that again!" But integrity and honesty are more than a game of "catch me if you can." "Honesty is the best policy," says the old truism; but the philosopher Immanuel Kant said, "Honesty is better than all policy."[13]

The problem in every generation of humans is that we do not value the truth highly enough. The "brothers," believers in the Jerusalem church led by James, shared this lack of understanding about the life of integrity God demands of His children. The words we speak as followers of Christ will either commend us to God or condemn us; James has made that clear. The word of a Christian must be dependable; his integrity must be unimpeachable.

Swearing Is Condemned (5:12)

"Above all, my brothers, do not swear—not by heaven or by earth or by anything else." "Above all" means "most importantly."[14] Why is this so important? James has discussed the believer's misuse of words on several topics: slandering other Christians, blaming believers for suffering, care for accuracy in teaching, words of real love, claims of faith and making verbal judgments about others. Why is avoiding swearing more important than any of these other topics?

James Adamson, in his commentary, writes, "Swearing is necessary only in a society where truth is not reverenced."[15] From Matthew 5:18 to 26:34, Jesus said thirty times, "I tell you the truth." God is a God of truth: "O Sovereign LORD, you are God! Your words are trustworthy, and you have promised these good things to your servant" (2 Samuel 7:28).

For James, salvation comes "through the word of truth" (James 1:18). A Christian who is apostate is said to have "wander[ed] from the truth" (5:19). Truth is a virtue held in the highest regard by God, by all of Scripture and particularly by James. Jesus Christ identified himself as the Truth in John 14:6 and is the truth personified in Ephesians 4:21.

But the truth is not always valued by men or their cultures. In his book *Against the Night,* Charles Colson cited an incident in which the President of Cornell University addressed a meeting of college educators at Harvard University and was challenged for suggesting that students' moral well-being should be given more attention.

Colson concluded, "Today, however, few educators—or any other leaders who shape public attitudes—have the audacity to challenge the prevailing assumption that there is no morally binding objective source of authority or truth above the individual."[16] This kind of relativism also seemed to characterize the Greek sense of truth. For the Greeks of James' time, truth was more intellectual than personal or moral.[17]

"Do not swear—not by heaven or by earth or by anything else" (James 5:12). To swear means "binding one's allegiance by invoking God's name as an assertion of one's truthfulness."[18] In present-day language, a person who would make a statement followed or preceded by "I swear to God" would be swearing or taking an oath in the strict sense of the original meaning here.

The Jewish culture of the first century evidently had two standards for truth.[19] The practice of making an oath when the speaker was intent upon being believed was perhaps more common than in present Western culture. But making oaths in daily speech is still practiced widely around the world. The implication of the oath is that the person who violated his oath would be punished more severely by God than the person who merely lied. This was the incentive to truthfulness when one took an oath.

Jesus expanded the prohibition of James beyond just making an oath in God's name. Matthew 5:33-37 says:

> Again, you have heard that it was said to the people long ago, "Do not break your oath, but keep the oaths you have made to the Lord." But I tell you, Do not swear at all: either by heaven, for it is God's throne; or by the earth, for it is his footstool; or by Jerusalem, for it is the city of the Great King. And do not swear by your head, for you cannot make even one hair white or black. Simply let your "Yes" be "Yes," and your "No," "No"; anything beyond this comes from the evil one.

Invoking the name of someone or of something the speaker holds as precious and swearing by his love for that person or thing is also forbidden.

Swearing always implies two standards for truth: a lower standard is in effect when just speaking in normal conversation, and the higher level of truthfulness when the believer swears. This is yet another example of the double-mindedness that characterized the Christians James was familiar with (James 1:8). Swearing was to them "more honest than other speech."[20] But a person of integrity, a righteous and holy person, has only one standard for truth. God has commanded in Leviticus 19:12, "Do not swear falsely by my name and so profane the name of your God. I am the LORD."

The heart of the problem can be framed in this question: Why should swearing be necessary for a follower of Christ who has the Spirit of Truth living within him? "Our mere word should be as utterly trustworthy as a signed document, legally correct and complete."[21]

Paul indicates in Second Corinthians 1:15-24 that God's promises are all true, all "Yes" and "Amen." They are never double-minded "yes *and* no" propositions. God's Spirit in believers forms and molds them in the likeness of Christ to create people of integrity whose word must be trustworthy and whose promises are completely dependable.

Think of all the promises God has made throughout human history. He promised Adam and Eve that the offspring of a woman would one day come to "crush" the serpent's head, and Christ came to destroy the power of hell and death. God promised that a Savior would be born and that He would one day become a sacrifice for the sins of the world; and the Father sent His only Son to live as a man and then to die as a sacrifice for sins (John 3:16). Although God did at times make an oath (Deuteronomy 4:31; 7:8; Hebrews 3:11; 4:3), the vast majority of His promises are just statements of what He intended or intends to do.

Swearing by someone or something greater than the speaker does not make the speaker more honest; it only associates the great person or the noble object with a potential liar. Taking oaths is actually commanded by God on rare occasions (i.e., Exodus 22:10-11). But promises to God and others are to be limited to those that believers actually can keep (Numbers 30:2; Leviticus 19:12, Zechariah 5:3-4).

The warning of this passage and the teaching of Christ is that oaths are not to be casually made, and in fact are not to be made at all. The reputation and integrity of a consistent Christian's life should be insurance enough that his statements can be trusted.

These prohibitions do not refer to the formal oath to tell the truth required in courtrooms or to the oath of office taken by politicians but to the normal daily communications of men and women in the course of their lives.[22] Some have taken this as license to avoid swearing allegiance to a flag or a country. The point of the passage is that God has condemned swearing casual oaths because they jeopardize the value that must be placed on complete truthfulness at all times. Swearing is condemned.

Integrity Is Commanded (5:12)

"Let your 'Yes' be yes, and your 'No,' no, or you will be condemned." Promises are statements of a Christian's intentions for the future and must be honored by the believer. Leviticus 19:11-12 commands, "Do not steal. Do not lie. Do not deceive one another. Do not swear falsely by my name."

Any statement of intention or commitment to a course of action commits the believer to follow through with the actions. Any statement of fact must be trustworthy in every detail. The deeper life is one that has renounced untruthfulness and exaggeration. "Therefore each of you must put off falsehood and speak truthfully to his neighbor, for we are all members of one body" (Ephesians 4:25). This is the new self, created to be like God in true righteousness and holiness.

Just saying, "I will be there Tuesday" or "You can count on me" obligates a believer to God and to the person to whom he has spoken. When asked to make a commitment, the mere use of the simple word “yes” is as binding as any oath or promise a believer could make.

The reader is challenged to ask himself, *What does my “Yes” really mean?* In common usage, it could mean “maybe, maybe not” or “if it is convenient and I don’t have a better offer” or “as long as I cannot find a really good excuse.” Or it could really mean “yes.”

James is using the present tense to indicate that the church to whom he wrote was already having problems with its integrity.[23] They made promises they did not keep. Their word could not be trusted unless they were made to swear they were telling the truth. Christians who say one thing and mean or do something else are living contradictions. This is precisely the problem the letter addresses. Christians who verbally professed love, faith and “true religion” were living at a much lower level of integrity than their words indicated. When they said “Yes” to Christ or “Yes” to other people, they meant something less.

Does your “No” mean no? Paul told Titus, “For the grace of God that brings salvation has appeared to all men. It teaches us to say ‘No’ to ungodliness and worldly passions, and to live self-controlled, upright and godly lives in this present age” (Titus 2:11-12). But the things these Christians had sought to expel from their lives were still present. Having promised God or a friend to never do some things again, they were still involved in them.

“God has said, ‘Never will I leave you; never will I forsake you’ ” (Hebrews 13:5). Our Lord had said “No” to the idea of ever leaving His followers alone to face the enemy and the world without divine help. The promise of a follower of Christ to put sin behind him must be as dependable as Christ's word. The believer has renounced deception and sin in favor of the life of the Holy Spirit. "Do not lie to each other, since you have taken off your old self with its practices" (Colossians 3:9).

The alternative to this life of integrity which God has commanded His followers to lead is judgment: "or you will be condemned" (James 5:12). Swearing by God obligates a person to a higher degree of guilt, putting him in greater danger.[24] Untruthfulness has its own measure of guilt. But involving the Father in an untruth by the mention of His name or the name of anything God has created adds a second offense, further condemning the untruthful.

God has given His followers power to tell and to live the truth, so that the world will believe the testimony of His saints. The integrity of the gospel rides upon the integrity of God's people in the eyes of a watching world. God is seeking truthful, sanctified Christians to represent Christ to a confused and lost world. "Do everything without complaining or arguing, so that you may become blameless and pure, children of God without fault in a crooked and depraved generation, in which you shine like stars in the universe as you hold out the word of life" (Philippians 2:14-16). Let your "Yes" mean yes and your "No" mean no.

Conclusion

Swearing is condemned in all its forms. When others do not believe you, rather than promising that you are telling the truth, ask God how you can live a better life of integrity so that others will believe your word.

Integrity is *commanded.* As a Christian, your veracity is a measure of the Lord you profess. Jesus Christ is the Truth. You are the visible representative of the truth of God to a world locked in darkness and spiritual deception. Be careful what you commit yourself to! Make no commitment unless you believe God is in it and you know He will help you deliver all you promise or more. That is certainly the way our Lord has behaved toward us. Let your "Yes" and your "No" be as trustworthy as the Lord you serve. You will "shine like stars in the universe as you hold out the word of life" (Philippians 2:15-16) in a world that has lost its integrity.

Questions for Reflection or Discussion

1. Do you, or does someone you know, have a habit of saying, "I swear" or "honestly"? Does this make people trust the speaker more or less? Why?
2. Is this text talking about the kind of swearing that involves four-letter words? Why or why not? What other texts in Scripture definitely address the use of vulgar language?
3. Why did Jesus forbid swearing by heaven, by earth, by the Holy City or by a person's own head (Matthew 5:33-37)? What is the message Christ was trying to communicate?
4. Why is this subject of Christian integrity so important to James? How does our credibility with words affect the rest of the Christian life?
5. Does your "Yes" mean yes when you commit

yourself to do something at home? at work? in church? Does your "No" really mean no when you make a commitment to avoid sinning? When is it most difficult to keep your commitments?

6. Why does "going beyond" simple truthfulness in daily speech condemn the speaker? To whom should you give promises or make vows? Under what circumstances is this wise?

Endnotes

1. Martin, *James,* 187.
2. Kittel, *TDNT*, vol. 4, 385-386.
3. Martin, *James*, 196.
4. A.B. Simpson, *Wholly Sanctified* (Camp Hill, PA: Christian Publications, 1991), 4.
5. Moo, *James*, 168.
6. Martin, *James,* 191.
7. Arndt and Gingrich, *A Greek-English Lexicon*, 766.
8. Davids, *Epistle of James,* 185.
9. Kittel, *TDNT*, vol. 4, 585-588.
10. William Barclay, *The Letters of James and Peter,* The Daily Study Bible Series, 2nd ed. (Philadelphia: Westminster, 1958), 125.
11. Martin, *James,* 195.
12. Adamson, *Epistle of James*, 192.
13. William J. Bennett, *The Book of Virtues* (New York: Simon & Schuster, 1993), 599-600.
14. S. Laws, *A Commentary on the Epistle of James* (San Francisco: Harper & Row, 1980), 219-220.
15. Adamson, *Epistle of James,* 194-195.
16. Colson, *Against the Night*, 44.
17. Douglas, *The New Bible Dictionary*, 1301.
18. Martin, *James,* 199.
19. Douglas, *The New Bible Dictionary*, 902.
20. Davids, *Epistle of James,* 190.
21. Mitton, *Epistle of St. James,* 193.

22. Moo, *James,* 174.
23. Martin, *James,* 204.
24. Ibid., 205.

Lesson 11

James 5:13-18

Healed and Empowered by Prayer

James 5:13-18

Is any one of you in trouble? He should pray. Is anyone happy? Let him sing songs of praise. Is any one of you sick? He should call the elders of the church to pray over him and anoint him with oil in the name of the Lord. And the prayer offered in faith will make the sick person well; the Lord will raise him up. If he has sinned, he will be forgiven. Therefore confess your sins to each other and pray for each other so that you may be healed. The prayer of a righteous man is powerful and effective.

Elijah was a man just like us. He prayed earnestly that it would not rain, and it did not rain on the land for three and a half years. Again he prayed, and the heavens gave rain, and the earth produced its crops.

What if medical science could develop a single cure for all diseases? Everything from depression to kidney stones to heart disease and cancer would be cured by this single miracle drug. As long as we are fantasizing, pretend that it is then discovered that this same medicine works even if a person is not ill to keep him healthy both physically and mentally. Would you take this medicine?

James is speaking to a normal congregation in abnormally difficult times. They are living in an occupied country, dominated by false religion and suffering persecution. These believers are ill, poor and confused. James has one answer, one antidote for all their situations: prayer. In these six verses, prayer is mentioned in every verse and applied to every circumstance.

Prayer Is the Answer to Life's Demands (5:13)

James begins with a question:[1] "Is any one of you in trouble?" (5:13). This particular word for trouble indicates "suffering some type of misfortune."[2] The word is not used for physical illness in this context. That type of affliction will be addressed in 5:14. The believers in the area of Jerusalem were "afflicted by hardship," probably resulting from persecution.[3] They were being pursued by persecutors like Saul, losing their homes, their property and even their lives. The answer to the question, "Is any one of you in trouble?" was undoubtedly "Yes!" for nearly all who read these words. But what should they do about it?

People often resort to prayer when there is trouble. Even people who would not ordinarily be considered praying people seem to understand that a crisis in their lives is an invitation to speak to God. I recall President George Bush calling evangelist Billy Graham to the White House to pray with him at the beginning of the Gulf War. King Hezekiah prayed when the Assyrians threatened to attack his kingdom and prayed again when his life was threatened by disease (2 Kings 18-20).

Most people, in trouble, do not need the command to pray. In fact, serious, mature Christians pray about everything. But some folks do need the command "he should pray" (James 5:13).

A pastor was listening to a person from his church give a long, anguished explanation of problems and intense emotions. Then the person with the life-threatening difficulties blurted out, "And don't tell me to pray about it; I'm in trouble here!"

Unfortunately, Christians facing "trials of many kinds" (1:2) must sometimes be commanded to pray. Prayer was the first choice of men of God in response to trouble. Paul counseled in Ephesians 6:18, "And pray in the Spirit on all occasions with all kinds of prayers and requests. With this in mind, be alert and always keep on praying for all the saints."

The believers James addressed were to pray not just for the removal of trouble, but for the strength and faith to faithfully endure it.[4]

The second question stands in sharp contrast to the first: "Is anyone happy?" (James 5:13). These two questions cover the gamut of human experiences: "in trouble . . . happy." The happiness described here is not necessarily resulting from good circumstances but is more descriptive of Christian joy in the reader's heart.[5] The same persecuted group of troubled people in the Jerusalem church could also be filled with "overflowing joy" (2 Corinthians 8:2).

One example of happiness and trouble coexisting in

the same moment is the unforgettable expression of pain and joy on a new mother's face after delivering a healthy baby. More than superficial fleeting happiness, believers who are filled with God's Spirit experience the joy of the Lord.

"Let him sing songs of praise" (James 5:13). Just as they were commanded to cry out to God in their distress, these saints are commanded to sing out to God in their times of joy. Colossians 3:16-17 commands:

> Let the word of Christ dwell in you richly as you teach and admonish one another with all wisdom, and as you sing psalms, hymns and spiritual songs with gratitude in your hearts to God. And whatever you do, whether in word or deed, do it all in the name of the Lord Jesus, giving thanks to God the Father through him.

God is the true source of all joy and of all deliverance. He must receive praise and glory from the lips and the lives of His people.

Singing prayers of gratitude, love and praise is commanded elsewhere in God's Word: Psalm 33:1-3 commands, "Sing joyfully to the LORD, you righteous; it is fitting for the upright to praise him. Praise the LORD with the harp; make music to him on the ten-stringed lyre. Sing to him a new song; play skillfully, and shout for joy." Prayer offered to God in the heat of battle or sung out in the cool, refreshing times of joy is the answer to life's demands.

Prayer Is the Antidote to Life's Diseases (5:14-16)

"Is any one of you sick? He should call the elders of

the church to pray over him and anoint him with oil in the name of the Lord" (5:14). "Sick" can mean "weakness of any kind," but James is referring to physical illness.[6] Being ill was common in the first century without modern medical care or knowledge of hygiene and proper diet. But even with today's medical care, Christians are often ill. When Christians are ill, whom should they call first?

Today, the first reflex of many of us is to call the doctor when we are ill. That is good, but it is not the best thing to do first. Our healing is more dependent upon God than medical science.

The first century also had doctors, but James commands that the ill person seek God's help first: "He should call the elders of the church to pray over him and anoint him with oil in the name of the Lord" (5:14). This commanded call (aorist imperative) for help from the church implies a sense of urgency. The person addressed may be too ill to go to the elders but well enough to initiate the process of prayer for healing by summoning the elders of the local church.

The elders are the spiritual leaders of the church. They held a special office in the churches of the New Testament. Paul "appoint[ed] elders in every town" (Titus 1:5). The churches called them "pastors" or "presbyters." Their calling was the pastoral care of God's people.[7] Not a pastor nor church leader nor "faith healer"—but rather a group of spiritual leaders from the local church was given the responsibility of prayer for the healing of the ill person under its care and authority.

This command has been obeyed in some church traditions from apostolic times until the present. Fearful of sensationalism and abuse by some, many churches have abandoned the biblical command to "call the elders of the church" and have them pray for people who are ill.

A history of The Christian and Missionary Alliance states, "The holiness movement also sparked renewed interest in the doctrine of divine healing—the direct intervention of God to restore health and wholeness to the physically sick."[8] In A.B. Simpson's church at the turn of the nineteenth century, healing services in which the elders of the congregation anointed and prayed for the sick became a regular part of the church's ministry.[9]

The elders of the church are to "pray over [a sick person] and anoint him with oil in the name of the Lord" (James 5:14). Unlike the commands in 5:13, where the believer prayed for himself, a group of spiritually mature elders are called to pray here. The circle of prayer is now enlarging. It is assumed that more than one elder or pastor will come to minister to the ill. Notice also that the call in this case is not generally given to just any Christian but to those chosen as spiritual leaders. All Christians should pray, but specifically, the elders must pray for the sick.

Their prayer is to be "in the name of the Lord," a phrase that means "according to the revealed character and purposes of Christ." The name of God represents all that God is and all He has promised to do. In Exodus 15:26, God gives His name as, "I am the LORD who heals you." It is the power and grace of God that will heal the person, not the virtue of those offering the prayer. These are not magical words but an indication of dependence upon Christ's healing grace. The name of Christ was associated with healing in the church of James' time (Acts 3:6-7; 9:34; 16:18). The authority to pray for healing has come from Christ and must always acknowledge that Christ is the focus of any prayer for healing (Matthew 10:1; Luke 9:1-6).

Anointing with oil could have at least two purposes: oil was used for medicinal purposes;[10] and oil was symbolic of God's blessing and of the Holy Spirit's presence in the life of the one anointed (Exodus 40:13-15; 1 Samuel 16:13).[11] David was anointed with oil by the prophet when he was chosen by God to be King of Israel "and from that day on the Spirit of the LORD came upon David in power."

It is doubtful that James, in 5:14-16, intended that the oil be used as a medicine, since the context is one of prayer and not the medical practices of the time.[12] The oil is symbolic of the Holy Spirit's presence and power in the healing of the ill believer.

The results of the church's obedience to these commands are restoration to health and forgiveness. "And the prayer offered in faith will make the sick person well; the Lord will raise him up" (5:15). The emphasis of this process is not upon the person who is sick, upon the prayer or upon the elders who are praying. The suffering patient is anointed "in the name of the Lord" and healed by the Lord. Jesus Christ is the focal point for the healing of the believer.[13]

The "prayer offered in faith will make the sick person well" (5:15). "Faith" means faith in Christ, the Lord, rather than belief in prayer or in the elders. As A.B. Simpson observed, Jesus Christ is the Lord for the body as well as for the soul.

Matthew 8:16-17 is a pivotal verse for this doctrine:

> When evening came, many who were demon-possessed were brought to him, and he drove out the spirits with a word and healed all the sick. This was to fulfill what was spoken through the prophet Isaiah:
>
> "He took up our infirmities
> and carried our diseases."

As Isaiah predicted (53:1-6), Christ died on the cross to redeem the whole man, both spiritual and physical.[14]

"The Lord will raise him up" (James 5:15). This verse is reminiscent of all the many times James must have witnessed Christ healing the sick and even raising the dead to life. Some theorize that this phrase refers to the resurrection, but the normal use of the verb is for recovery from illness or physical healing.

God gives spiritual healing too. "If he has sinned, he will be forgiven. Therefore confess your sins to each other and pray for each other so that you may be healed. The prayer of a righteous man is powerful and effective" (5:15-16). James allows the possibility that some sickness is related to sin (see also 1 Corinthians 11:27-31). But not all sickness is the result of sin. Job (Job 1:8) and Lazarus (John 11:4) are examples of men who were ill so that God would be glorified through their healing.[15]

When sickness is accompanied by sin, that sin must be confessed in order for the ill person to be healed. The spiritual health and physical health of the believer must never be treated as independent of one another. Christ is faithful to those who come humbly to admit and repent of their faults: "If we confess our sins, he is faithful and just and will forgive us our sins and purify us from all unrighteousness" (1 John 1:9).

Confession is to be made to God and "each other," not to a religious professional. The elders are not mentioned in this context. Confession was important to the life of the early church.[16] Notice that the circle of prayer has now grown to the level of the whole body of Christ as individual believers join in praying. Prayer is now commanded for the whole congregation: "pray for each other" (James 5:16). Healing involves the whole church in prayer. Prayer and confession are privileges and responsibilities of the whole church rather than the sole property of a privileged few.

"The prayer of a righteous man is powerful and effective" (5:16). Those who are without faith in Christ (1:7) or who are motivated by selfish desires (4:3) will not receive the answers they long for from God. Those who refuse to ask God are also among the unrighteous who suffer from a frustrated prayer life. The knowing sinner goes unanswered.

But the saint of God, a righteous man, will be heard. Who is this man? He is any Christian living a consistent life of holiness in God's strength. He can pray powerfully and effectively. The text indicates that a sinner who has repented can pray for healing and be heard by a gracious God. These are not people who have never sinned but praying sinners who have repented.

What does "powerful and effective" imply? Richard Foster has said,

> Prayer catapults us onto the frontier of the spiritual life. Of all the Spiritual Disciplines prayer is the most central because it ushers us into perpetual communion with the Father. To pray is to change. Prayer is the central avenue God uses to transform us.[17]

Foster goes on to illustrate the powerful effects of prayer in the lives of "all who walked with God" like Jesus, David, Martin Luther, John Wesley, David Brainerd, George Fox and Adoniram Judson. They all prayed as if God would change the world in response to their petitions. The effectiveness of prayer is illustrated by what God accomplished through their lives.

Prayer Is the Anticipation of Life's Deliverance (5:17-18)

"Elijah was a man just like us. He prayed earnestly that it would not rain, and it did not rain on the land for three and a half years. Again he prayed, and the heavens gave rain, and the earth produced its crops" (5:17-18). Any ordinary believer can pray with power and effectiveness. The life of this great Old Testament prophet of God illustrates the point.

Elijah was just a man of faith who suffered the same limitations as any one of those who read this letter.[18] His life story, some of which is told in First Kings 17-18, included facing persecution, false religion and personal suffering, much like James' readers faced. Elijah bravely stood his ground for God on Mt. Carmel against the Baal prophets and then fled from the threats of a single politically powerful woman. He fearlessly faced death and then begged to die in a moment of doubt and loneliness. Elijah was just a man with fears and failures, but more than that, a man who prayed and trusted God in faith.

He "prayed earnestly" (James 5:17). "In prayer he prayed" is the idiom[19] used in the original, indicating that Elijah prayed intensely and with persistent faith. God moved heaven and earth at this ordinary man's extraordinary request: "He prayed earnestly that it would not rain, and it did not rain on the land for three and a half years" (5:17). God certainly granted this righteous man a powerful, effective answer to his petitions.

"Again he prayed, and the heavens gave rain, and the earth produced its crops" (5:18). He refused to give up, praying seven times for rain that had not fallen in three and a half years at his request from God. Why did he continue to pray? He believed in God's love and power. He prayed "in the name of God," according to the Father's will. The harvests that brought life back to the land and to the people of God were waiting upon a single ordinary man who believed in God and therefore exercised the powerful effective weapon of believing prayer.

Conclusion

The subject of this section of James is prayer. Prayer is the answer to life's demands, the antidote for life's diseases and the anticipation of life's deliverance. What blessing are you seeking from God? Do you need physical healing, a job, a home, guidance from God? Pray!

What blessing are you thankful for? Sing praises to

God; lift the name of the Giver of "every good and perfect gift" (1:17) up to heaven in songs of praise.

When you are ill, call the elders of the church to pray for you and to anoint you with oil in the name of the Lord. If you have sinned, then confess and repent. Jesus Christ died to forgive and to heal you, to make you both whole and holy.

Pray for one another and be accountable to one another as you confess your sins rather than hiding or rationalizing them. God longs to cleanse you and make you righteous. He has called the entire church family to work and pray together to reach this goal of Christlikeness.

Prayer is the most powerful weapon God has given to His Church. Every blessing awaits ordinary, repentant believers who will come to the Lord in faith: "You do not have, because you do not ask God" (4:2). Pray like Elijah and watch the horizon for God's effective, powerful response of deliverance, healing and a bumper crop of life.

Questions for Reflection or Discussion

1. Why is prayer the proper first response in hardship or trouble? Which is better: to ask for immediate removal of the trouble or for faith to persevere? How does this relate to what James said in chapter 1 about troubles and trials?
2. How should we pray when we experience joy? How is joy possible in suffering? How does "singing songs of praise" differ from just speaking to God?
3. Is there a conflict between faith in God's healing power through Christ and seeking medical help?

Why do you think James calls for the elders of the church to pray rather than the church in general? How does your church follow this command?

4. What is the purpose of the anointing oil used in the prayer of healing for the sick? What did oil symbolize in the Old Testament?
5. What kind of faith is needed to pray for healing? How does repentance relate to the process of healing? How does Christ's atoning work (Matthew 8:16-17) relate to healing? How might sickness be related to sin? What is the relationship between physical and spiritual well-being?
6. Do you truly believe God can answer the prayer of a righteous man (or woman)? Can you give examples of ordinary people with extraordinary prayer lives?

Endnotes

1. Ropes, *Saint James*, 303.
2. Arndt and Gingrich, *A Greek-English Lexicon*, 398.
3. Martin, *James*, 205.
4. Arndt and Gingrich, *A Greek-English Lexicon*, 397.
5. Moo, *James*, 175.
6. Davids, *Epistle of James*, 192.
7. Moo, *James*, 176.
8. Robert Niklaus, John S. Sawin and Samuel J. Stoez, *All for Jesus* (Camp Hill, PA: Christian Publications, 1986), 32.
9. Ibid., 55.
10. Davids, *Epistle of James*, 193.
11. Moo, *James*, 179-181.
12. Keith M. Bailey, *The Children's Bread* (Camp Hill, PA: Christian Publications, 1977), 137-138.
13. Adamson, *Epistle of James*, 198.
14. Drake Travis, *Christ Our Healer Today* (Camp Hill, PA: Chris-

tian Publications, 1996) is an excellent resource for the subject of healing ministry in the Church and the theology of healing.

15. Kittel, *TDNT*, vol. 2, 337.
16. Davids, *Epistle of James*, 195.
17. Richard J. Foster, *Celebration of Discipline* (San Francisco: Harper & Row, 1988, revised), 33-34.
18. Adamson, *Epistle of James*, 200.
19. Martin, *James*, 212.

Lesson 12

James 5:19-20

Section A

Reconciled by Loving Intervention

James 5:19-20

My brothers, if one of you should wander from the truth and someone should bring him back, remember this: Whoever turns a sinner from the error of his way will save him from death and cover over a multitude of sins.

The previous lesson focused the reader's attention on prayer to save the lives of believers who were physically ill or spiritually ill. The power and effectiveness of prayer as a spiritual weapon for every situation was made clear. The sinning believer was invited to confess his sin so that the church could pray for his restoration, his life. But what of the sinner who does not come to Christ in repentance for healing? In this final lesson, James concluded the letter with the strongest possible words of warning and exhortation. What are Christians to do when faced with the double-minded, inconsistent state of their faith and of their lives? How can we help those who struggle and fail to live the deeper life that God desires?

Early in my walk with the Lord, I nearly strayed from the truth. I met a teacher who insisted that there is no hell, no place of suffering where men are separated from God and goodness for eternity. My teacher passionately and convincingly argued that a loving God would never create a place like hell. When I was nearly convinced of this lie, my brother spoke to me about my error. He gently encouraged me to read the four Gospels to see what Jesus said about this subject. I was compelled to believe the teachings of Christ and to renounce the false doctrine I had been so tempted to adopt.

My brother's intervention in my life at that moment kept me from making a terrible error in my young Christian life that would have taken me outside the circle of biblical Christianity and into the world of cults and people who deny the faith. When believers wander from the truth, Christ has a plan for their restoration to His Church. The plan involves loving intervention from their spiritual family. The deeper life demands a love that gets involved and takes responsibility for the welfare and spiritual health of the family of God.

Brothers Can Miss the Way of Truth (5:19)

James is once again speaking to "brothers"—Christians: "My brothers, if one of you should wander from the truth . . ." He has already mentioned the possibility of self-deception on the part of followers of Christ:

"Do not merely listen to the word, and so deceive yourselves. Do what it says" (1:22). One form of "wandering from the truth" involves the sin of knowing the truth and choosing not to apply it to daily living (1:22). This problem of a sterile knowledge of Scripture which produces no fruit of loving action or righteous living seemed to be prevalent in the church to whom James addressed his letter (1:26; 2:8, 12, 14; 3:13).

The theme of self-deception is not unique to James. Paul said, "Do not deceive yourselves. If any one of you thinks he is wise by the standards of this age, he should become a 'fool' so that he may become wise" (1 Corinthians 3:18). James also indicated that those who considered themselves "religious" (James 1:26) or "wise and understanding" (3:13) needed more than empty claims to validate their grasp of the truth. Only a holy life would verify such claims. Otherwise, they had "wandered from the truth," however sincerely they believed their professions.

The central theme of James' whole letter comes across here:[1] "If one of you should wander from the truth . . ." The "truth" is that *a Christian life existing only in the mind and vocabulary of the believer is not the life of faith Christ intended.* These believers have wandered away from the intention of God for their lives.[2]

The choice of the word "wander" indicates that the wanderer has not accidentally or unconsciously moved from the truth, but intentionally departed from the way Christ and the apostles have taught and modeled in their own lives. They have thrown their moral compass overboard and are navigating through life blindly—perhaps the devil (3:6, 15) is doing the steering.

These professed believers knowingly eliminated the teachings of Christ that did not appeal to them. If, after reviewing the teaching of Christ concerning the plight of the lost, I had continued to insist that there is no hell, I would have committed this error. Or if, knowing of James' commands for the treatment of the poor brother, I continue to show prejudice to favor the more powerful brother, I am an apostate who has knowingly wandered from the truth.

Christians are also deceived by others. In 1:16 James said this, and Paul agrees, "I tell you this so that no one may deceive you by fine-sounding arguments" (Colossians 2:4). Brothers are at times led astray by sincere but false teachers. Or they are enticed by the teachings of their fallen culture: "They have left the straight way and wandered off to follow the way of Balaam son of Beor, who loved the wages of wickedness" (2 Peter 2:15). Those who "wander from the truth" (James 5:19) were too common in James' church.

Christians must be warned that "truth is something that must be *done* as well as believed."[3] In Judaism (Psalm 25:4-5; 26:3) and in Christ's teaching (i.e., Matthew 22:16; John 3:21; 14:6), truth is as much in a person's lifestyle as in what he thinks or professes. Brothers can miss the way of truth.

Brothers Who Lose Their Way Can Return (5:19)

". . . and someone should bring him back." Those brothers who have wandered from the truth must turn back to a life of obedience and faith. Having professed faithfulness but taking another path, Peter denied that he knew Jesus Christ. In a moment of fear, he publicly renounced his relationship with the Lord.

Predicting this wandering from the faith, Jesus had said to him, "Simon, Simon, Satan has asked to sift you as wheat. But I have prayed for you, Simon, that your faith may not fail. And when you have turned back, strengthen your brothers" (Luke 22:31-32). Peter needed to be brought back to faith that produces faithfulness.

Those who wander from the truth are in danger! "Sin . . . gives birth to death" (James 1:15). The sense of urgency is real. The warnings of the book for those who merely hear the teaching of God in Scripture without making any change in their behavior apply to the wayward brother. Paul wrote to brothers in Rome warning that the "wages of sin is death" (Romans 6:23): death for those who follow their example and never really believe, and death for one who has no genuine faith in Christ to produce the fruit of a righteous life (James 2:14).[4]

Are these "brothers" really among those redeemed through faith in Christ? Professions of faith without any faithfulness call their eternal life into question (1:20). James has stated that such faith is useless. He warned those whose lives contradict their words: friends of the world are enemies of God (4:4). John has expanded the teaching here to say, "If we claim to have fellowship with him yet walk in the darkness, we lie and do not live by the truth" (1 John 1:6).

The deeper life that God desires is a life that faith produces. For James, this is no time to play theological percentages or word games to assume that those who have wandered away from the truth are fine without any action on the part of the faithful. The time for action from those who really love them has come.

The people of the church are called to find these spiritual nomads living in their barren, fruitless deserts and to bring them back to "the righteous life that God desires" (James 1:20). Notice that the person who wandered away is not given the primary responsibility for his return.[5] The "someone" who must bring that person back is still in the church and in close fellowship with God.

"Brothers, if someone is caught in a sin, you who are spiritual should restore him gently." This is what my brother did when I nearly wandered away from the truth. "But watch yourself, or you also may be tempted" (Galatians 6:1-2).

Notice the need for gentleness and humility in Paul's instruction to those who lovingly confront a person who has departed from the truth. Spiritual people display spiritual fruit in returning the wayward saint and in redeeming those who only thought they had expressed true faith.

Jesus addressed the process of restoration and reconciliation for offending brothers in Matthew 18:15-20. The process of restoring sinning Christians to fellowship acknowledges that some will do offensive, sinful things. A plan of reconciliation is necessary for maintaining relationships between believers and for restoring those who depart from the way of truth.

James was speaking to suffering, persecuted believers who would be tempted to take the easy road in the face of opposition from their Jewish culture and their pagan Roman government.[6] When they were faced with the pressures of trials and temptations, they were tempted to compromise or even to desert the church and fall away from their fellowship with other believers rather than persevering (James 1:2-3). Led by the Holy Spirit, James insists that someone is needed to encourage and bring them back.

The responsibility of the person who lives a righteous life is to care for the "weaker brother" who is tempted and failing (Acts 20:35; Romans 14:1; 15:1; 1 Corinthians 9:22; 1 Thessalonians 5:14). Love demands action to rescue the person who is wandering away from the truth. The intervention of a spiritual person can be effective. James has indicated that one of God's people can successfully bring these apostates back to the way of truth. Brothers can return those who lose their way.

Brothers Can Rescue the Lives of Their Wayward Friends (5:20)

"Remember this: Whoever turns a sinner from the error of his way will save him from death and cover over a multitude of sins" (5:20). The final word of James to his Jewish brothers scattered among the churches is still a word of preaching rather than a parting greeting. New Testament letters normally end in greetings, but not this one. His words of urgent exhortation to the people of God continue to the last sentence.

"Remember this. . . ." Readers are to pay close attention to the final instruction of the letter. James has sought to correct many false practices in his listeners: sins of the tongue, false religion, prejudice, materialism and pride are among their problems. Those who had not wandered away in these areas probably knew someone who had.

Most Christians hate confrontation. Unfortunately,

there is a minority in the faith who look forward to conflict (4:1). James rebuked selfishness and contentiousness. But now he encourages a form of righteous confrontation.

Christians are to be willing to risk a friendship or rejection or the anger of another person if their brothers' lives are in danger. "Sinners" were all around James' readers every day. Like people in a lifeboat who will not ask anyone else to enter, they were allowing their friends and neighbors to drown all around them, lost in a sea of confusion.

"Whoever turns a sinner from the error of his way will save him from death" (5:20). This phrase closely follows Ezekiel 33:11 and Proverbs 10:12. The original phrase "will save his eternal soul from death"[7] moves the warning from the threat of mere physical consequences to the realm of eternal ones. Souls are at risk here! Eternal death and hell are the fate we are seeking to avoid for the "sinner."[8]

A "sinner from the error of his way" is an unsaved person. This differentiates him from the brother who has wandered from the truth; the "someone" involved in the process of rescuing the lost one[9] in need of salvation is now involved with a second kind of problem.

For the person of faith, knowing the difference between a brother who has wandered from the truth and a sinner who never really embraced the truth can be difficult or impossible. All the fruit of their lives can appear the same or be so inconsistent (James 3:9-12) that they are unrecognizable as Christians. They can repeat the same words concerning a professed faith without any genuine transformation of their lives (2:17).

Both groups need the intervention of believers in order to bring them into the deeper life God has called them to live in Christ. Even if it is a different judgment, both groups are still in danger of God's judgment if they do not repent in faith and walk in righteousness with the Spirit of God.

God has a reward for these rescuing heroes and a great benefit for the victims of error they reach: They "will save [the victim] from death and cover over a multitude of sins" (5:20). The lost person will inherit new life and be spiritually born again when he repents of his sin and places his faith in Christ (1:18, 21). His life will be saved from eternal death and separation from God. The wayward believer will be restored to fellowship with God and effective fruitful faith. As in First John 1:9, his sins will be forgiven and he will be cleansed from unrighteousness.

There has been some question of whose sins are covered, those of the sinner or the rescuing saint. Scriptures are cited to support both points of view. Proverbs 10:12 says, "Love covers over all wrongs." The "covering of sins" implies forgiveness: "Blessed are they whose transgressions are forgiven, whose sins are covered" (Romans 4:7; see also Psalm 32:1-2).

Some theorize that the Christian who brings people to faith and reconciliation with God is forgiven here.[10] But this is unlikely, because the person who is spiritual is the one who will restore the sinner. The spiritual person is already forgiven through his faith in Christ. The soul saved and the sins covered are those of the sinner who is turned to God.[11]

James' words do not imply that the rescuer loses his reward. "Watch your life and doctrine closely. Persevere in them, because if you do, you will save both yourself and your hearers" (1 Timothy 4:16). The hint here is that those who obey this urgent call to seek out the lost and the wandering to bring them to God will be blessed for their good work.

The love that covers a multitude of sins and brings wayward brothers back to God is the love of Christ. The life that bears this kind of spiritual fruit will be eternally rewarded (Matthew 25:31-46; James 2:14-26). "The righteous life that God desires" (1:20), the deeper life of the Spirit, is one that is outreach-oriented. Christ has called every believer to seek and to save the lost just as He did.

Conclusion

Revival and reformation are needed in the evangelical church at the end of the twentieth century. Many recent books, like *The Body* by Charles Colson (Word Publishing, 1992) and *No Place for Truth* by David Wells (Eerdmans, 1993) point to the falling away of North American evangelicals from New Testament practice and belief. Os Guinness and John Seel edited *No God But God: Breaking with the Idols of Our Age*, a book which powerfully challenges the Church's adoption of our world's modern culture as the newest idolatry.

Eighty-five percent of North Americans claim to be "Christians," but we behave and believe like pagans. As Guinness and Seel say, "There has been a carelessness about Christian orthodoxy, a corruption of Christian obedience, a vacuum of Christian leadership. Much of the public face of 'American Christianity' is a stunning testament to the power of religion without God."[12]

Christians who believe one thing and do another are present in every generation. Though studies reveal that church attendees believe that being drunk or high is a sin, they report in alarming numbers that they regularly do this anyway. Believers who disapprove of sexually explicit movies and magazines view them anyway. Those who profess to know Christ also engage in sex outside of marriage, cheat on their taxes or lie to their employers.

Have you wandered from the truth? Does your life contradict your beliefs? Come back to Christ in repentance today. Return to the only life God created you to live, a life of holiness and righteousness. Expel any idols from your life that have taken the place of Jesus Christ as your Lord.

Christian, do you know someone who has strayed from the faith? Do not wait for the whole church to find out or for the elders or pastoral staff to go and ask the person to come back to fellowship and holy living; *you* go and "bring him back." "Remember this: Whoever turns a sinner from the error of his way will save him from death and cover over a multitude of sins" (James 5:20).

Armed with the truth God has given us in the book of James, you can be a redemptive influence in the world. Your prayers are powerful and effective when you offer them (5:16). Choose to live "the righteous life that God desires" (1:20) and help others to live it too!

Questions for Reflection or Discussion

1. How common is it for Christians to wander from the truth? Is it more common for them to wander from the truth in their understanding of biblical

teaching or in their practice of it? Is this more common today than in James' day or less? Why?

2. Why do you think James did not specify that elders should be the ones who seek out those who wander from the truth? Do the indefinite pronouns "someone" and "whoever" have any significance? If so, what?
3. Which is more difficult for you: evangelism of those who are unchurched or seeking to restore professing believers whose lives contradict their profession? Why? What can you and your church do to obey this command that "someone should bring him back"?
4. How can the person who has "wander[ed] from the truth" (5:19) be identified? Who is qualified to make this judgment?
5. What rewards await the person who reaches wandering brothers and brings them back? What is the reward of those who turn sinners from the error of their ways to a life of faith and righteousness in Christ? How are you currently involved in these two types of outreach? How could you become involved?

Section B

Conclusion

The conclusion of the book of James answers the question, "What should we do in response to this truth from God?" God has spoken; the church must respond to the accusations and the exhortations of James.

The major themes of the letter flow along the river of applied righteousness in the life of God's people. Faith, prejudice, love, mercy, righteous communication, submission to God's plan and sovereignty, suffering, persecution and patience until Christ's return require that God's truth be filled out in the muscle and sinew of the body of Christ.

The church of our century must respond like those who heard Peter preaching in Acts 2:14-37: "When the people heard this, they were cut to the heart and said to Peter and the other apostles, 'Brothers, what shall we do?' " (2:37).

James opens the life of the church up to the standard of God. This righteous church leader describes the deeper life of the Spirit in everyday terms so that its characteristics are easy to see in an individual life or in the life of a church. The contrast between his life and lives of his hearers was stark even though he indicated that "we all stumble in many ways" (James 3:2).

The men and women of the church to whom James wrote were, like many Christians around the world today, suffering persecution. The temptation to compromise or to vacate the faith that produces such different and holy lives is present in every difficult circumstance of life. But in the face of suffering for doing good, the temptation is great to live a kind of innocuous Christian life that seemingly neither really harms nor helps anyone.

We can find in the Church of every generation the double-minded man who looks into the mirror of God's truth only to see nothing memorable. The simulated, sterile faith that fails to transform professed believers into the image of a holy, loving Christ had produced a kind of hybrid disciple of Christ by the time James was writing to his fellow Jewish believers.

These "brothers" spoke of faith but did not live by faith. Their inconsistent works and their unloving, judgmental and prejudicial actions belied lives that were affected little by their faith. The neglect of the poor and the helpless widows and orphans of their age spoke more loudly than their insistence that they were Christ's followers. His disciples are identified by the way they love one another.

The love of God, which is the heart of the deeper life, the "Christ life," as A.B. Simpson called it in his book by the same title,[13] compelled James to send his dear brothers this letter of exhortation. God still loves them; it is not too late to repent and live as God desires.

Simpson, writing about the book of James, said, "Compromise with the world is unfaithfulness to Christ and adultery in His sight. It is in this connection that our text is introduced. 'The spirit he caused to live in us envies intensely' (James 4:5). He is constantly guarding our loyalty of heart and our single and unqualified devotion to Christ alone."[14] The chapter is titled "God's Jealous Love." The love of God embodied in the presence of the indwelling Holy Spirit calls the Church back to faithfulness and holiness through the letter of James.

The God of grace who had called these Christians to become His children, the God who "chose to give us birth through the word of truth, that we might be a kind of firstfruits of all he created" (1:18), is calling His children to behave and believe like children of God. The call to healing prayer in the final chapter is an invitation to the double-minded Church to return to Christ in repentance for spiritual and physical healing.

How should we respond to this word from the Lord? We must respond like Josiah did when the Book of the Law was found in the temple after so many years of neglect and disobedience by the people of God (2 Chronicles 34:14-33). We must repent on our knees with tears and remove all the detestable idols of our age from the life of the church. Os Guinness observed in *No God But God:*

> As on the occasion of Martin Luther's ninety-five theses in the sixteenth century and Soren Kierkegaard's single thesis in the nineteenth century, Christendom is becoming a betrayal of the Christian faith of the New Testament. To pretend otherwise is either to be blind or to appear to be making a fool of God. The main burden of this book is a direct challenge to the modern idols of evangelicalism.[15]

Books like those written by Charles Colson are calling the Church to be the Church, to live holy, sacrificial lives consistent with the Word of God.[16] For such a day, the book of James was written. May God grant its readers the grace to live as He desires: in righteousness, living faith, love and true holiness.

Endnotes

1. Davids, *Epistle of James,* 198.
2. Kittel, *TDNT,* vol. 5, 49-53.
3. Moo, *James,* 189.
4. A.W. Tozer, *The Pursuit of God* (Camp Hill, PA: Christian Publications, 1982), 12-13.
5. Martin, *James,* 219.
6. Ibid., 218-221.
7. C.F.D. Moule, *An Idiom Book of New Testament Greek* (London: Cambridge University Press, 1959), 185.
8. Martin, *James,* 219.
9. Mayor, *Epistle of James,* 492.
10. Dibelius, *James,* 259-260.
11. Moo, *James,* 190.
12. Os Guinness and John Seel, *No God But God*, 12.
13. A.B. Simpson, *The Christ Life* (Camp Hill, PA: Christian Publications, 1980).
14. A.B. Simpson, *The Holy Spirit* (Camp Hill, PA: Christian Publications, 1994), 520.
15. Guinness and Seel, *No God But God*, 10.
16. Colson, *The Body,* 29-49.

Selected Bibliography

Works on James

Adamson, James. *The Epistle of James.* The New International Commentary on the New Testament. Grand Rapids, MI: Eerdmans, 1976.

Barclay, William. *The Letters of James and Peter.* The Daily Study Bible Series, 2nd ed. Philadelphia: Westminster, 1958.

Davids, Peter. *The Epistle of James.* The New International Greek Testament Commentary. Grand Rapids, MI: William B. Eerdmans Publishing Co., 1982.

Dibelius, Martin. *James: Hermeneia—A Critical and Historical Commentary on the Bible.* Philadelphia: Fortress Press, 1975.

Hort, F.J.A. *The Epistle of St. James.* London, 1909.

King, Guy H. *A Belief That Behaves: An Expositional Study of James.* Fort Washington, PA: Christian Literature Crusade, 1970.

Laws, S. *A Commentary on the Epistle of James.* San Francisco: Harper & Row, 1980.

Manton, Thomas. *James.* Geneva Series of Commentaries. Carlisle, PA: Banner of Truth, 1988 (first printed, 1693).

Martin, Ralph P. *James.* Word Biblical Commentary. Waco, TX: Word Inc., 1988.

Mayor, Joseph B. *The Epistle of James.* Grand Rapids, MI: Kregel Publications, Inc., 1990 (first printed: London, Macmillan, 1913).

Mitton, C.L. *The Epistle of St. James.* London: Eerdmans, 1966.

Moo, James. *James.* Tyndale New Testament Commentary, Revised. Grand Rapids, MI: Eerdmans, 1987.

Ropes, James H. *Saint James: Critical and Exegetical Commentary.* The International Critical Commentary Series. Edinburgh: T & T Clark, 1991.

Simpson, A.B. *James* in The Christ in the Bible Commentary Series, vol. 6. Camp Hill, PA: Christian Publications, 1994.

General Works Cited

Anderson, Neil T. *The Bondage Breaker.* Eugene, OR: Harvest House Publishers, 1990.

Arndt, William G. and Gingrich, F. Wilbur. *A Greek-English Lexicon of the New Testament.* A translation and adaptation of Walter Bauer's German lexicon. London: The University of Chicago Press, 1957.

Bailey, Keith M. *The Children's Bread.* Camp Hill, PA: Christian Publications, 1977.

Barna, George. *The Frog in the Kettle.* Ventura, CA: Regal Books, 1990.

Bennett, William J. *The Book of Virtues.* New York: Simon & Schuster, 1993.

Colson, Charles. *Against the Night.* Ann Arbor, MI: Servant Publications, 1989.

________. *The Body.* Dallas: Word Publishing, 1992.

Douglas, J.D. (editor). *The New Bible Dictionary.* Grand Rapids, MI: Eerdmans, 1962.

Foster, Richard. *Celebration of Discipline.* San Francisco: Harper & Row, 1988, revised.

Gallup, George, Jr. *Religion in America.* Princeton, NJ: PPRC, 1990.

Guinness, Os, and Seel, John. *No God But God.* Chicago: Moody Press, 1992.

Hybels, Bill, and Wilkins, Rob. *Descending into Greatness.* Grand Rapids, MI: Zondervan Publishing House, 1993.

Keener, Craig S. *Bible Background Commentary.* Downers Grove, IL: InterVarsity Press, 1993.

Kittel, Gerhard and Friedrich, Gerhard. *Theological Dictionary of the New Testament.* Grand Rapids, MI: Eerdmans, 1964.

Lean, Garth. *Strangely Warmed.* Wheaton, IL: Tyndale House, 1964.

Lewis, C.S. *The Problem of Pain.* New York: MacMillan, 1962.

Marshall, Paul. *Their Blood Cries Out.* Dallas: Word Books, 1997.

Moule, C.F.D. *An Idiom Book of New Testament Greek.* London: Cambridge University Press, 1959.

Niklaus, Robert, Sawin, John S. and Stoez, Samuel J. *All for Jesus.* Camp Hill, PA: Christian Publications, 1986.

Sider, Ronald. *Rich Christians in an Age of Hunger.* Downers Grove, IL: InterVarsity Press, 1977.

Simpson, A.B. *The Christ-Life.* Camp Hill, PA: Christian Publications, 1980.

_______. *The Fourfold Gospel.* Camp Hill, PA: Christian Publications, 1984.

_______. *The Holy Spirit.* Camp Hill, PA: Christian Publications, 1994.

_______. *Wholly Sanctified.* Camp Hill, PA: Christian Publications, 1991.

Tam, Stanley. *God Owns My Business.* Camp Hill, PA: Christian Publications, 1969.

Tozer, A.W. "Five Vows for Spiritual Power." Camp Hill, PA: Christian Publications, 1996.

_______. *The Pursuit of God* Camp Hill, PA: Christian Publications, 1982, 1993.

_______. *The Pursuit of Man.* Camp Hill, PA: Christian Publications, 1998.

Travis, Drake. *Christ Our Healer Today.* Camp Hill, PA: Christian Publications, 1996.

Wells, David F. *No Place for Truth or Whatever Happened to Evangelical Theology?* Grand Rapids, MI: Eerdmans, 1993.

Wesley, John. *A Plain Account of Christian Perfection.* Kansas City: Beacon Hill Press, 1966.

_______. *Wesley's 52 Standard Sermons.* Salem, OH: Convention Book Store, 1967.

Young, Edward J. *Thy Word Is Truth.* Grand Rapids, MI: Eerdmans, 1957.